Rescued from Darkness

A Powerful, Practical Life-Guide For New Christian Believers

The How-To's of Changing Your Life & Living for God

Foreword by the late Dr. Bill Bright
Founder, Campus Crusade for Christ

LISA CLAY

xulon PRESS

Foreword

Lisa, I am very impressed with your book, *Rescued from Darkness*, and I am happy to extend the following endorsement:

"There is a pressing need for a book like this!

Rescued from Darkness has 50 concise chapters focusing on Biblical issues which new believers in the 21st century must understand to be foundationally established in their spiritual walk.

It is an innovative, power-packed discipling tool for this generation's convert, a resource with great potential for believers at every stage of their walk with Christ, yet finely tuned for those who are newcomers to Christianity.

The magnitude of spiritual illiteracy in our world requires a practical yet bold approach to "grounding" people in God's ways. *Rescued* brings a fresh and compelling discipling approach to believers who will use it as a guide.

November 19, 2002
Dr. Bill R. Bright
Founder and Chairman, Campus Crusade for Christ

100 Lake Heart Drive
Orlando, Florida 32832

Table of Contents

Why I Wrote "Rescued from Darkness"

I was 20 years old before I heard the truth about eternal life. I was a sophomore at Ohio University in Athens, Ohio, and a baseball player named Mike Olejarz invited me to church. I told him I already had a 'religion' and wasn't interested.

Mike wasn't satisfied with a 'no,' and kept bugging me until I finally relented and promised to go.

It was springtime, and I wore a polka-dot navy dress to church. I had no idea that my life was about to change forever!

The church, New Life Assembly of God, was on South Green. Pastor John Palmer had pioneered it, hoping to impact college students at O.U.

I sat in a simple metal folding chair, and watched as they passed Kentucky Fried Chicken buckets for the offering. It was the most casual offering I'd ever seen!

Pastor John delivered the sermon (he's a great teacher-preacher), and for the first time in my life I understood that I had sinned against a Holy God, but that He made a way to forgive me by sending Jesus to take all the punishment for my sin.

Somewhere in the core of my being I knew I was hearing the truth about Jesus Christ.

When Pastor John gave the altar call, I stood up and responded. I figured there was no sense messing around when the truth was confronting me face-to-face!

A young man named Rich was the campus pastor, and he prayed with me that day to receive Christ as my savior. I had no idea that God would intertwine our lives forever! He would become my husband 2 years later.

From that moment, it seemed a powerful energy entered my

life. I realized I had a purpose and meaning for being alive! I had found hope, and I had found God. Really, He had found <u>me</u>.

That was 23 years ago. Since then I have been living my life in Christ's service.

There are so many people out there who are living life like I was. They are totally ignorant of the truth about Jesus. I wrote this book for them.

I wrote this book for believers who have just begun their new life in Christ, and who need mentoring in many basic issues of the Christian life.

I also was inspired to write this book for Christians who have been believers in Christ for a long time, but have never learned to live out the practical truths of the gospel in their everyday lives.

Because God rescued me from the darkness of my sin, I owe it to Him to do everything I can to help rescue others, and train them to become successful, joy-filled, Christ-honoring, dedicated believers.

I commit this book to my friend Jesus, who loves me deeply. I honor and glorify you Lord. Use this book to bring many souls to your kingdom, and to train those who are new Christians, so they might in turn lead others to your love.

Lisa Clay

Acknowledgments

God has used many people to launch this book, and they deserve tremendous credit.

My husband Rich and my two supportive boys Jared and Wesley make life worth living. All three of you are the apples of my eye. I dearly love you.

My mother has always said I would be a writer. She was right. I love you mom.

Ruby Stump, my administrative assistant, worked countless computer hours during this project. Way to go Ruby! You are a blessing.

Brenda Mitchell, a deep, heart-felt thank you for listening to the voice of the Spirit. Be supremely blessed!

Grandpa, I'm so sorry you didn't live long enough to see my book published. You were so proud to share your writer's mantle with your grand-daughter. But you accepted Christ as your savior, and I will see you again in heaven.

Dr. Bill Bright, you will never know what our meeting did for me. I felt the presence of Jesus Christ in you like I never have in any other person. I was, and am now, completely humbled by your life.

Dr. James O. Davis, thank you so much for your help on this project.

Dr. George O. Wood, you are a favorite of ours! Your kind words meant so much.

May you all experience the fruits and blessings that come with supporting God's work.

What This Book Will Do For You

So you want to know God? Good. He <u>wants</u> you to know Him!

In each short chapter of this book you will discover something new about God and about living your life as a Christian.

What will you find in the chapters?

1. Powerful, practical instruction about almost every part of your life: friends, your money, your job, anger, supernatural power, your thought life, addictions, prayer, angels, recognizing right from wrong, the devil, racial unity, sin, hope, sex, loyalty and heaven are a few of the topics covered.

2. At the top of each chapter is a verse from the book of Colossians in the Bible. It was written by a man named Paul, a man who once put Christians in prison, but was radically changed by a powerful encounter with Jesus Christ! The scriptures are taken out of "The Message" Bible, so you'll have no problem understanding what the Bible has to say about issues.

3. At the end of each short chapter are two helpful sections:

> ❖ **"GET A BETTER GRIP"** directs you to scriptures you should look up in your own Bible for more information on the subject in that chapter.

> ❖ **INTERACTIVE SECTION** with questions designed to allow you to write down what God is saying to you personally. (Yes, He wants to speak to you personally!)

<u>What else can you expect to receive from this book?</u>

1. It will help you understand God's plan for you.

2. It will advance your growth in Christ at a faster rate.

3. It will answer many of your questions about living a Christian life.

4. It will explain what God thinks about real life issues you struggle with.

Chapter 1

You Can Be Changed!
(Leave your past behind)
Colossians 1:1-2

"I, Paul, have been sent on special assignment by Christ as part of God's master plan. Together with my friend Timothy, I greet the Christians and stalwart followers of Christ who live in Colosse. May everything good from God our Father be yours!"

Paul had hated Christians! His name before he became a Christian was Saul, and he was a 'religious' man who thought he was doing God's work by hunting down Christians and having them thrown in prison and killed. In spite of all this, God had a great plan to transform Saul and use him to impact the whole world.

One day Saul was riding a donkey to the city of Damascus to arrest more Christians, and a brilliant light from heaven flashed around him, knocking him to the ground. A voice called out to him, "Saul, Saul, why are you out to get me? I am Jesus, the one you are hunting down!" (The Message)

Instantly Saul was blinded and could see nothing. He followed Jesus' orders to go into the city, and a Christian named Ananias received a command from the Lord to place his hands upon Saul's eyes to heal him of his blindness. Something like scales fell off Saul's eyes, and his sight was miraculously restored!

Saul then accepted Jesus as his savior and God, was baptized in water, and immediately began to preach and teach that Jesus was indeed the messiah. The Christian believers began to call him Paul, probably to indicate that the man "Saul" had been completely changed into a new man!

Within a few short years, Paul became a strong leader, traveling all over the Roman world to preach the truth that Jesus could save people from their sins.

Because of the immense change in his life, he made many enemies. Most of those enemies were 'religious' people who were threatened and jealous of people following Jesus instead of following their religious traditions.

Paul ended up in prison because of his beliefs and his preaching. It is from this prison in Rome that Paul writes a letter to the Christian believers in the city of Colosse.

Even though these Christians had accepted Christ as the son of God and the Savior of the world, they had been listening to false spiritual teachings from men who were only interested in gaining a following for themselves.

When Paul heard that these dangerous and untrue teachings had swept into the Colossian church, he was alarmed. He knew that satan, the devil, was trying to lead these believers astray into lifestyles and practices that would separate them from God and the truth of His Word.

The Colossians were also struggling with issues in their daily lives, many of the same kinds of issues we deal with in our lives today. Paul decided the best way to help the Colossians was to write them a letter dealing with the difficulties and temptations they were facing.

He immediately began to write, warning them to stay away from false teachers and their empty philosophies. He filled his letter with helpful and encouraging teaching so the Colossians would understand how to change their lives through Christ's power.

Each word of this letter was inspired by God Himself to train Christians how to live their lives for Jesus and show them how to distinguish between good and evil. Even though God used Paul to write the words down, the Holy Spirit living inside Paul gave him the words to say.

This letter was saved and collected together with other writings God had supernaturally inspired His chosen messengers to record. We call this collection the Bible.

The Bible is also called the 'Word of God,' and is the most unique book on the earth. Because it is literally the power of God formed into words and sentences, it contains supernatural ability to deliver people from the prison of sin.

If you are being held captive by some kind of sin, and you know you are messing up your life, you need God's Word to set you free. Like Paul, who was sinning against God, perhaps you have sinned against God and need to ask for His forgiveness.

You can ask God right now, right where you are sitting, to forgive you for living a life of sin, and ask Him to enter your heart and make you a new person. God did it for 'Saul,' re-creating him into the powerful man of God called 'Paul,' and He'll do the same thing for you.

You don't have to live in a prison of sin, misery and depression anymore. You can be free!

If you've already asked Jesus to be your Savior, you've begun your new life. Just like the Colossian Christians, you also need instruction and help to grow strong in your new life in Christ.

You can make it with Jesus! He'll transform you, deliver you from your past and create for you a fresh future, filled with hope and joy.

Paul turned out to be a powerhouse for God! His past was gone forever, and he became a brand new man, serving God and ministering to other people. And even though he wrote this letter to the Colossians from a Roman prison, in his soul and spirit Paul was a free man.

God has big plans for your life, too! Look ahead with joy, because no matter where God takes you, you can expect great things to happen!

<u>GET A BETTER GRIP by reading:</u>
Acts 9:1-31   2 Corinthians 5:17

What did God speak to me today through this chapter?

What action do I need to take in my life to apply what I have learned?

Chapter 2

Welcome To The Family!
(Relationships in God's family)
Colossians 1:3-5

"Our prayers for you are always spilling over into thanksgivings. We can't quit thanking God our Father and Jesus our Messiah for you! We keep getting reports on your steady faith in Christ, our Jesus, and the love you continuously extend to all Christians. The lines of purpose in your lives never grow slack, tightly tied as they are to your future in heaven, kept taut by hope. The Message is as true among you today as when you first heard it. It doesn't diminish or weaken over time."

Maybe you're like Eric. He grew up in a single parent home, and his mom had to work long hours to keep the family going. Eric always felt like he was missing something, but didn't want to spend too much time thinking about it. When Eric was 17, his friend invited him to an "Extreme Life" youth night at his church. For the first time in his life, Eric heard that Jesus Christ loved him and accepted him.

That night, Eric's life changed forever. He met Justin and Adam, two new friends who became like brothers. Brian and Debbie Lawson, a Christian married couple, took a personal interest in Eric, having him over to their home for cook-outs and swimming. Eric found what he'd been missing, and it wasn't long before his mother and he had been welcomed and embraced into a loving family.

Did you grow up in a dysfunctional or hurtful family? In today's world it is hard to find people who have experienced the joy of being part of a loving, godly family.

When you get saved (you've accepted Jesus as your Savior) God makes a way for you to have an instant new family or community to hang out with, one which you can safely love and who will show you wholesome love.

God will enable you to love and forgive your biological family, and it may be possible to restore a good, pure relationship with them. But He also provided a Christian family so you can learn how to grow and prosper and be a success at serving Jesus.

Being a new part of the family of God is really exciting! You can build relationships with other Christians as you attend church and become involved.

God wants to show you what true love is by introducing you to Christian people who can love you with a clean love, a love that you've probably never experienced before.

One of the most powerful and comforting things about being a Christian is that you can go to other believers to pray for you and with you, connecting you together in the kingdom of God.

People who really love Jesus want to help you understand that you can trust Him for all the needs you have in your life. You can do that by praying with one another. Praying with other believers teaches you how to communicate easily with your friend Jesus, and how to pray in faith and not doubt. It's also a great way to make close friends who will love you and care for you.

God wants you to be an active part of His family. He wants you to learn right ways to build relationships and he wants to help you get rid of things in your life that are hurting your ability to keep healthy relationships.

You can do this by going to one church regularly and getting to know the people there. They will love you and help you to succeed! And God will see to it that you meet the right friends, the ones who will stick with you as you grow spiritually, helping you all the way.

If you need a family, God has already planned a way for you to have a good one. Don't spend any more time grieving about the family you didn't have, because He's designed a new family for you!

The key is this: you have to be with your new family to get to know them. So don't delay, get to a Bible-believing, Bible-teaching church right away and meet your new relatives!

GET A BETTER GRIP by reading:

Acts 2:42-47   Psalm 68:5-6   Roman 8:15

What did God speak to me today through this chapter?

What action do I need to take in my life to apply what I have learned?

Chapter 3

Truth is Alive and Well

Colossians 1:6

"It's the same all over the world. The Message bears fruit and gets larger and stronger, just as it has in you. From the very first day you heard and recognized the truth of what God is doing, you've been hungry for more."

The luxury ship 'Titanic' received several warnings to slow down and watch for icebergs. The ship's crew ignored the truth and steamed ahead, smashing into an iceberg and sinking into the Atlantic on April 14, 1912.

New scientific evidence has revealed that when the Titanic was built, too much glass was mixed in with the iron, which caused the ship's rivets to weaken. When the ship hit the iceberg the rivets broke apart, allowing water to pour into the hull. The mighty Titanic now lies at the bottom of the ocean, rusting away so quickly scientists say it will almost disappear in 40 years.

The Titanic disaster seems like the perfect picture of what is happening to our world today. Many members of the media, politicians, professors, religious figures and scientists claim there is no absolute, pure truth, and they continue to try to remake our culture by encouraging everyone to do what is right in their own mind, mixing up right with wrong and creating a formula for disaster.

As a result, instead of steaming ahead, our culture is becoming weaker and weaker. Many people are lost in a maze of emotional problems, mental problems, and family failures.

Without truth to guide and strengthen us, we are headed for that final, dangerous collision with an 'iceberg,' a tragedy we cannot fix, and because we are weakened from living life without God's truth, we will sink, just like the Titanic.

The good news is that we don't have to sink! There is One God of Truth, and He wants to rescue each one of us and teach us how to live and operate in the truth. If you are sick and tired of living a lie, of deceiving others and being deceived yourself, hold on tight! What you <u>are</u> about to hear is truth, and it's gonna blow your mind!

There is a God of truth, and there are also a lot of false 'gods.' So, which is which and how can you be sure you are serving the one True God? What about Buddhism? Hinduism? Islam? Hari Krishna? What about their claims to be 'true religions?'

All these so-called 'gods' make demands on their servants to somehow earn a place in their heaven by following a set of strict and rigid guidelines. These demands must be met in order for the follower to have even a vague hope of being accepted. And after all their work, none of these religious followers are convinced they will gain entrance into heaven! Their lives are lived in anxiety and guilt, hoping against hope to somehow be 'good enough' to avoid hell!

In sharp contrast, the one true God, the Father of Jesus Christ, operates in love and mercy. He sent His only Son to the earth (leaving his perfect and powerful place in heaven) in order to carry mankind's sins to the cross and make a way for all people to be saved and go to heaven.

The one true God needed justice. Human beings were filled with sin and all types of wickedness, and God is holy and upright. Since he could not bring sinful human beings to live in heaven (a place of perfection and cleanness) he sent Jesus to be a "sin cleanser" so that all those who accepted his gift offer of eternal life would be able to enter heaven. Billy Graham once said "It is strange that we prepare for everything except meeting God."

What a terrible thing it will be for some people to arrive at

Judgment Day and learn that they have spent their entire lives serving a 'god' of demands and regulations, and still they do not have a place in heaven.

No other god can rescue you from eternal hell, no other god loved you enough to send His own son to be punished for your sin, no other god operates in grace, mercy and forgiveness. Only the <u>one true God and Jesus Christ His son love like that.</u>

God the Father is the only God who actually fills you with His spirit so that you can overcome all the hardships and temptations of the world. He wants you to succeed! He is not looking to find fault with you!

How can you know for certain that this is the truth? Jesus Himself testified to it when He declared, "I am the way, the truth and the life. No one comes to the Father except through me." And then He proved it by rising from the dead!

In the deepest parts of your heart the Spirit of God will witness to you that this statement is true. Jesus is the only way to get to God, the only way to be assured you are going to heaven, the only way to be saved. Stop and listen to your heart!

Just as Colossians 1:6 says, this same truth, the good news that Jesus saves, is being preached around the world and is growing and producing many believers in the one true God.

Truth is still alive and well, because it lives on through Jesus Christ and through every one who believes in Him.

If you want to discover more truths, begin reading your Bible every day. The Lord will teach you and train you until you are satisfied in your soul that truth is not "what people want it to be." On the contrary, truth is clearly spelled out in the pages of God's Word.

Break out of the lies and the cover-ups that deny Truth exists. Truth is a person, and that person is Jesus Christ. He testified about Himself, saying "I am the way, the <u>Truth</u> and the life."

GET A BETTER GRIP by reading:
John 6:47   John 7:28-29   2 Thessalonians 2:10

What did God speak to me today through this chapter?

What action do I need to take in my life to apply what I have learned?

Chapter 4

Now That I'm a Christian, What Am I Supposed to Do with My Life?
Colossians 1:7-8

"It's as vigorous in you now as when you learned it from our friend and close associate Epaphras. He is one reliable worker for Christ! I could always depend on him. He's the one who told us how thoroughly love had been worked into your lives by the Spirit."

So, you're SAVED! You want to be a radical for God! That's great! When your life changes so dramatically, it's awesome and you want to tell everyone about it.

Now you're probably thinking "Does this mean I need to be a pastor, or in full time ministry?" Well, God <u>does</u> have a tremendous plan for your life, and you do need to find out what that plan is.

If you are 'called' to be a pastor, evangelist, or in full time ministry (that means if God has chosen you to do that job) there are several things you will probably notice in your life:

1. You have a burning desire to share the gospel (the good news of Jesus) with anybody who will listen.

2. Other career goals in your life now seem unimportant and

insignificant compared to letting people know about how they can be saved.

3. You have a hunger to know God through His Word, and you feel constantly compelled to share what you are learning.

4. When you spend time in prayer about being in full time ministry God confirms that 'calling' to your spirit by encouraging you and leading you in that direction.

5. Mature Christians confirm your call into full time Christian service.

6. You sense a continual tug on your heart from the Holy Spirit to serve Him, laying aside other goals you may have had prior to that.

Everyone who becomes a Christian is commanded to share the truth about Jesus Christ with lost people. All Christians are to be in 'ministry', but there are some Christians who are called out to devote their entire life's work to spreading the gospel by becoming full time ministers.

If this is your calling, God will make that clear to you as you spend time with Him. If you are called to be a plumber for Jesus, or an electrician or an attorney for Christ, those are also valuable and important jobs! God needs every one of us to be faithful in the vocation He has selected for us. If each one of us shares Jesus with the people we meet at work, God's kingdom will grow by leaps and bounds.

Full time ministry is a tremendous calling, but it's not the only 'job' in the kingdom of God. Most new believers are excited about their new life in Christ, and want everyone else to know the hope Jesus has given them. This doesn't necessarily mean you are called to be in full time ministry.

God will help you understand what He wants you to do with your life! Don't become discouraged, just trust Him to lead you as the days and months go by. You are so very valuable to Him! He wants to reveal His plans for you, but most of the time those plans are unveiled slowly instead of revealed instantly.

Simply trust God to help you see what He wants you to do with your life! He might bring huge changes to your plans for yourself, or He may just encourage you to stay at your current job and be a dynamic witness for his son Jesus.

Whatever He asks you to do, one thing is true. If you serve Him wholeheartedly, He will cause you to be a success in everything you put your hands to!

GET A BETTER GRIP by reading:
2 Peter 1:10   Romans 12:2

What did God speak to me today through this chapter?

What action do I need to take in my life to apply what I have learned?

Chapter 5

How Can I Know God's Will?

Colossians 1:9

"Be assured that from the first day we heard of you, we haven't stopped praying for you, asking God to give you wise minds and spirits attuned to his will, and so acquire a thorough understanding of the ways in which God works."

Choices and changes. Are you afraid of making wrong moves and ending up in a mess? Do you know that you can be free of the fear of making bad decisions by calling out to God to help you make right choices?

In the past you were probably used to making decisions based on what seemed right to you. Now you have a divine guide who is always available to you and always willing to give you spiritual wisdom and understanding.

When you face a puzzling set of circumstances, instead of scratching your head or worrying, simply ASK God to help you and bring you an answer!

Some people get impatient and can't seem to wait for God to show them what to do. They go ahead and act on their own and create bigger problems for themselves.

This scripture promises that if you keep praying God will fill you with the knowledge of His will! Usually that means that He will cause you to understand the way He is leading you by ordering circumstances or coordinating situations to let you know which choice is right for you.

For example, if you are praying about whether or not to accept a certain job, God may cause people and situations and scriptures to come your way that will all line up and point to one specific direction.

For a while it may seem confusing, and you may wonder whether you can hear from God at all! But He will make sure that your searching heart finds the right path.

You can be sure of this, God will never lead you in a direction that is against what is written in His Word, the Bible. For instance, if you are wondering whether or not to enter into a relationship with a married man or woman, you can stop wondering! God's Word says, "Do not commit adultery. Do not be deceived; adulterers will not inherit the kingdom of God." (I Corinthians 6:9-10)

God WANTS you to know His will. He is not hiding it or making it difficult to understand. He is not playing games with you to see if you can guess correctly.

He has a perfect plan for your life, and He wants you to know which paths to choose so that you can fulfill that plan.

It may take some time before you are sure you know God's will. He is training you to trust Him and to learn to wait patiently. One important thing to remember: when God does reveal His will to you, and it is confirmed, He expects you to be immediately obedient and follow His directions. Once you do, it will be easier to determine God's will in other areas of your life as well.

Don't ever give up seeking God's plans. Once you are confident you are walking in His will it will bring you years of joy and fulfillment.

GET A BETTER GRIP by reading:
Ephesians 5:15-21   Psalm 143:10

What did God speak to me today through this chapter?

What action do I need to take in my life to apply what I have learned?

Chapter 6

I Want to Please My Heavenly Father!
(How do I do it?)
Colossians 1:10-12

"We pray that you'll live well for the Master, making him proud of you as you work hard in his orchard. As you learn more and more how God works, you will learn how to do your work. We pray that you'll have the strength to stick it out over the long haul—not the grim strength of gritting your teeth but the glory-strength God gives. It is strength that endures the unendurable and spills over into joy, thanking the Father who makes us strong enough to take part in everything bright and beautiful that he has for us."

Have you ever known someone who was impossible to please? They operate in a negative lifestyle, hoping someday to find something that will make them happy and live up to their expectations. You may have had a parent like that. Perhaps it was your father, and you can't imagine a father who would be pleased with you just because he loves you.

But there IS a Father who accepts you and loves you! He is pleased with you because you have believed in His Son Jesus. Your heavenly Father is pleased that you have faith! That's right, it's FAITH that makes God happy and pleases Him. Loving Jesus and dedicating your life to serving Him is what your new life is all about. And because you love Him and want to please Him, you need to understand the many things that delight His heart.

Repentance is one of those things. When you repented of your sin and accepted Jesus as your Savior, it meant that ALL your past sins were washed away. But sin is a fact of life on this earth, and even in your best efforts you will fail and commit sin.

All Jesus wants you to do is bring your failure to him, confess it and turn away from your sin. He will forgive you and give you strength to resist that sin. Repentance pleases God and keeps you close to Him.

It also pleases God when you strive to live a pure life. Ask Him for grace and mercy to help you overcome impure or immoral temptations. He won't look down on you or condemn you for being tempted. Like a loving father, He sees you when you are about to fall and comes running to help you! He's not a growling presence, lurking over your shoulder waiting for you to make a mistake so He can blast you. He's full of kindness and strength, and nothing makes Him happier than helping one of his children avoid pitfalls.

It also pleases God when you do good works, like buying groceries for widows or helping a poor family fix their house. When you do good deeds, it helps you understand who God is and how much He loves people. It also strips away selfishness in your life and allows you to be more like Jesus.

It pleases God when you endure hardships and still remain loyal to Him. It delights God's heart when you patiently wait for Him to work out details in your life instead of trying to work them out yourself.

It pleases God when you praise and thank Him even when life is tough!

You can please God by simply acknowledging His presence. When you get up in the morning and say, "Lord, I'm sure glad you are here with me!" you give God tender pleasure.

Believing God answers prayer is another way to please the Lord. Living a life of faith means asking God to meet your needs and then trusting Him to do so. When you choose to BELIEVE God for healing, for financial help, for emotional strength and for all the other needs in your life you are really saying "God, I KNOW that you are the Almighty and that you have my entire life in your hands. I know you won't fail me and you will provide for me in one way or another!"

To sum it all up, if you want to please God, just believe in Him and love Him with all your heart, mind, will, emotions, and strength and then serve Him in humility all of your days. He'll give you the help you need to please Him, because He's the source of every good work in your life!

GET A BETTER GRIP by reading:
Hebrews 11:62   Corinthians 5:7-9   Proverbs 15:8
Ecclesiastes 2:26

What did God speak to me today through this chapter?

What action do I need to take in my life to apply what I have learned?

Chapter 7

Rescued From Darkness
(From sin-slave to freedom)
Colossians 1:13-14

"God rescued us from dead-end alleys and dark dungeons. He's set us up in the kingdom of the Son he loves so much, the Son who got us out of the pit we were in, got rid of the sins we were doomed to keep repeating."

The "Star Wars" movie episode "Return of the Jedi" has a great scene. The evil lord Darth Vader and his boss, the wicked emperor, have ruled the galaxy for generations. But Luke Skywalker has become a powerful Jedi knight and has defeated the 'dark side.'

Moments before the explosion of the emperor's battle station, the 'Death Star,' Luke cradles the dying Darth Vader in his arms, because he has discovered Vader is his father.

"Father, I've got to save you!" Luke says.

"You already have, Luke, you already have," whispers Darth Vader in his dying moment.

Although Vader dedicated most of his life to serving the 'dark side,' he was rescued by the love of a son who would not give up on him. He was snatched out of the clutches of darkness and returned to the light.

Sound familiar? It's the story of your life! You were also rescued by the love of The Son! You used to be a prisoner of the devil, bound by his chains of darkness, wearing the mask of evil. You took orders from satan just like Darth Vader took orders from the wicked emperor. You were a slave, a victim of the enemy of your soul.

Then Jesus appeared on the scene, a heavenly warrior released from above to explode into the darkness of your life and destroy the work of the devil! He set you free and restored you, giving you hope for a bright and awesome future.

You are forever free from the power of satan and from his rule and control over your life! No longer do you have to be fearful or scared, because sin is no longer your master. Jesus Christ the Son of God has removed you from the domain (the authority and power) of wickedness and has moved you into his kingdom of light and love.

God has pardoned you and will not force you to pay any penalty for your life of sin. The forgiveness God gives you through Jesus is complete.

And not only are you forgiven, but God has made you a full-fledged son or daughter, which means that you are granted an inheritance.

Just exactly what have you inherited? It's rich, man, rich! The right to call upon Jesus, the king of the universe, for any help, anytime! The right to request anything at all from God the Father (everything from finances to a Christian wife or husband!) The right to live in freedom from fear, bondage, hatred and addictions. The right to hope, the right to love, the right to go to heaven when you die. You are rich! Unbelievably, undeniably rich!

You have it all! Now thank God, and keep thanking him, because there is no other power great enough to rescue like that. And there is no other name under heaven given to men by which we must be saved. The name of Jesus is the ultimate authority in heaven, on earth and under the earth.

GET A BETTER GRIP by reading:

Hebrews 2:14-15   Hebrews 9:15   Ephesians 1:18-21
Romans 6:14

What did God speak to me today through this chapter?

What action do I need to take in my life to apply what I have learned?

Chapter 8

God Rules!

Colossians 1:15-17

"We look at this Son and see the God who cannot be seen. We look at this Son and see God's original purpose in everything created. For everything, absolutely everything, above and below, visible and invisible, rank after rank after rank of angels—everything got started in him and finds its purpose in him. He was there before any of it came into existence and holds it all together right up to this moment."

"If God is real, why doesn't he show himself to me?" Many people ask that question because they are frustrated with an 'invisible God.' Some folks just cannot trust what they cannot see!

That becomes an ironic argument in this techno-powered world, however, because virtual reality is something one can see, hear and experience, but it isn't REAL.

Jesus Christ came to earth to make God visible to people. The Bible says, "He who has seen Me (Jesus) has seen the Father." (John 14:9) God wanted to show sinful, doubting humans His loving-kindness by allowing us to see an exact representation of His being. Everything Jesus did was to please and honor His Father so that the world could discover God through Him.

Jesus Christ is God, and was with God the Father in the

beginning. When it was time to create the universe, the galaxies, the earth and mankind, Jesus was designated the head architect, and he created all things through his power and authority.

Creation has an order and structure delicately organized to sustain living things. Contrary to false, human-invented teaching, life did not evolve, nor was it a haphazard accident! Jesus Christ is the author of life and He is the only one who can effectively rule and preserve life. He is the king and ruler over all creation to this day, no matter who believes it and who doesn't!

Until the time comes for created things to come to an end, God the Father and his son Jesus reign from heaven. Evil still has freedom to work and to cause destruction, but evil is also restrained and limited by the hand of God. If not for God's protection and intervention, evil would prevail and mankind would be forever lost.

In fact, God was the one who created the angels who rebelled against him and became demons! The devil, their leader in this rebellion, is also a created being. So even though these evil angels rebelled and brought their wickedness to earth to try to destroy humans (who were God's greatest creation) God is still the ultimate ruler over them all.

Certain religions claim that Jesus was just a good teacher and a great man, but that he was simply a man and not God. That would mean that he was created by God and was not the creator. That is absolutely not true; a great man and a good teacher would never blatantly lie and lead people to believe that he was God's Son when he was not.

All things in heaven and earth, in the universe and beyond, hold together because Jesus causes it to be so through His mighty and powerful Word. One word from Jesus' mouth is powerful enough to create or to disintegrate!

By His Words he created all things, visible and invisible, and someday through His words Jesus will bring all things to an end. And when that happens, you and I will be saved because we have believed in His Word which says

"Salvation is found in no one else, for there is no other name under heaven given to men by which we must be saved." (Acts 4:12)

GET A BETTER GRIP by reading:

Philippians 2:10   Hebrews 1:1-4   John 1:1-5

What did God speak to me today through this chapter?

What action do I need to take in my life to apply what I have learned?

Chapter 9

You Are Now a Body Part
(You're a vital part of God's body, the church)
Colossians 1:18-19

"And when it comes to the church, he organizes and holds it together, like a head does a body. He was supreme in the beginning and—leading the resurrection parade—he is supreme in the end. From beginning to end he's there, towering far above everything, everyone. So spacious is he, so roomy, that everything of God finds its proper place in him without crowding."

Have you ever seen a human head floating down the street without a body under it? Of course not! Can you imagine someone without a mouth trying to eat a hamburger? No way! Think about how freaky it would be to have a pair of legs walk by you in the mall parking lot (legs without a body attached!)

If you're a head, a mouth, or a pair of legs, you need a whole body to hang out with! It's just like that when you give your life to Jesus. Suddenly, you are a body part! You are a very important part of what's called the 'body of Christ,' which Jesus himself called the 'church.'

All believers in Jesus are collectively referred to as the 'church.' The church is not a building, a structure or a denomination. It is a living 'body' with Jesus as the head of that body. Each believer is a part of that living body. And just like your body has different names and uses for its individual parts (eye, leg, knee), each believer has different gifts and functions in the body of Christ.

You are a vitally important part of the church, and you have a specific job to do in order to maintain a healthy, functioning body! Imagine for a moment that your hand suddenly decided it wasn't going to do its job anymore. Think about how much more difficult everything would be without your hand! It is the same in the body of Christ if you are missing or not fulfilling your function, because then the body (the church) is crippled in some way.

You have a unique contribution to make in the body of believers. You have a ministry, a service, an assignment from God to complete while on earth. Maybe God has designed you to be a helper . . . to assist people in certain tasks in the church.

Perhaps you are gifted to teach a Sunday school class, greet people in the foyer, sing in the choir, visit prison inmates, be a youth leader.

There are so many different roles in the body of Christ, and each person has been gifted by God to serve in their own role.

How can you find out what 'body part' you are? Simply examine the talents and abilities you have and begin to use them for the kingdom of God. If you are an actor, use your gifts in the church drama department. If you have the ability to fund-raise, use it to help raise money for missions!

One very important point: You need to understand the role of Jesus and the role of the leadership of the church. Jesus is the head. He gives the orders and directs the entire body. When the whole church is following the head, everybody is healthy and the body is under control.

God has given pastors to each 'body' to help that body stay on track. A pastor is sort of like a personal trainer who helps develop the body to keep it strong, training it to function at its peak. The pastor is given the duty of caring for the body, praying for it when it is hurt and helping it through struggles. The pastor is a gift to the body to help it grow and prosper.

The pastor is also the spiritual authority in the church. A pastor seeks the Lord and then gives the body direction. It is very important that you honor and recognize the role of pastor, and that you listen to their instructions and do your best to carry out those instructions.

The pastor must answer to God for the leadership he or she gives to the body, and the body must answer to God for the way they follow the leadership of the pastor.

Now that you know that you are a body part, get moving! Get involved in your church using the talents and gifts God has given you. The body of Christ can't function in fullness until you are a working part! And just like your human body, the more you exercise your body part, the stronger it will become!

GET A BETTER GRIP by reading:
Romans 12:4,8   I Corinthians 12:12-31

What did God speak to me today through this chapter?

What action do I need to take in my life to apply what I have learned?

Chapter 10

Only Type 'C' Blood Can Save You
(The power of the blood of Jesus)
Colossians 1:20

> "Not only that, but all the broken and dislocated pieces of the
> universe-people and things, animals and atoms-get properly
> fixed and fit together in vibrant harmonies, all because of his
> death, his blood that poured down from the Cross."

I started to panic, and then I started to scream! Blood squirted everywhere-MY blood! I had a terrible accident when I was 13 years old. A drinking glass shattered in my hand severing most of my left thumb. My father whisked me into the car, rushed me into the emergency room, and watched while they sewed my thumb back together.

Fortunately, I had not lost enough blood to require a transfusion. Have you ever been wounded and lost a lot of blood? If you were taken to the emergency room perhaps you received a blood transfusion that saved your life. Your life is in your blood, and if you did not have blood your body would die quickly.

We are alive because we have life-giving blood running through our bodies, carrying nourishment into our cells and toxic wastes out of our cells.

We also live in the spirit realm because of blood . . . the blood of

Jesus! Jesus offered Himself up to die in our place to pay for our wickedness, and His sacrifice wasn't easy. The Roman soldiers stripped the skin off His back with a whip, and then wove some long thorns into a circle and shoved it onto his skull. He was forced to carry a hard, heavy wooden cross through the streets of Jerusalem, and then was nailed with sharp spikes to that cross.

Jesus lost a great deal of blood from his tortured body, and that very blood is what God used to 'cover' our sins, so that when He sees us, He sees the blood and sacrifice of His son instead of seeing our wicked and rebellious ways.

Jesus' valuable, priceless, God-type blood is the purchase price for lost sinners. Any other substance would never have been effective in covering and cleansing our sins!

Our spiritual life, literally, is in and through the blood of Jesus, which carries out the toxic wastes (sins) and brings fresh, healthy nourishment to our hurting soul.

When you accept Jesus Christ as savior, Jesus' blood sacrifice brings you into a peaceful relationship with God. You don't have to fear death or going to hell anymore. God has made a way for you to be with him forever, and that is through the pricey, perfect blood of His Son.

You've been covered in 'Type C Blood," (Christ's Blood) which means simply that His blood has and will continue to cleanse you of sin. You have constant access to this powerful blood, so you can pray over your family "Lord, I cover them with your blood as a protection from the devil, as a healing ointment for their health, as a covering for their sin, and as a reminder of the hope they have in Jesus."

There is only ONE blood that has the power to save you from your sins, and it's not the blood of animals or the blood of humans. The blood that <u>saves</u> is Type C blood. <u>Christ's blood alone</u> has authority in heaven and on earth to bring salvation to anyone who will believe.

There is a sacred time set aside to remember the awesome sacrifice Jesus made for us. It's called 'communion.' Usually grape juice and a piece of bread are used to represent Jesus' blood and body. Jesus commanded that believers should eat and drink these to remember what He did for us on the cross, and to remind ourselves that He is alive and will return someday to get us.

You can never thank God enough for the power of the blood of Jesus.

GET A BETTER GRIP by reading:

I Peter 1:18-19   Ephesians 1:7   I Corinthians 11:23-32

What did God speak to me today through this chapter?

What action do I need to take in my life to apply what I have learned?

Chapter 11

Changing Your Mind Changes Your Life
(Renewing your thoughts)
Colossians 1:21

"You yourselves are a case study of what he does. At one time you all had your backs turned to God, thinking rebellious thoughts of him, giving him trouble every chance you got."

If you desire radical change in your life, the first thing you must start with is your mind. When you lived a sinful life, your mind and thoughts were hostile to God and God's ways. You were not able to please God because of your sinful behavior. Your mind was constantly dwelling on corrupt and wicked thoughts, and you resisted godly counsel and instruction.

Now that you are a Christian, God's Word tells you to exchange your old, nasty thoughts for new thoughts and a new mind set! No longer do you have to live with harsh, hateful and malicious thoughts toward yourself and others. Those thoughts led you to do evil things, things that you are now ashamed of. But now it is possible to <u>change</u> your thought life, thinking wholesome and positive thoughts.

God wants you to re-learn how to <u>think!</u> When corrupt and awful thoughts enter your mind you must refuse to entertain those thoughts. Let me give you an example:

What would you do if you were in a grocery store wheeling your cart around, and a man dressed in black started grabbing things off the shelves and slamming them into your cart? What if he began to force your cart to the checkout line, filled with junk you didn't even want? What if he began sneering at you and saying "You WILL eat this food that I'm forcing you to buy!"

I know what I would do! I'd say "Get away from me! You can't force me to put these things in my cart, and I refuse to buy them! Get lost, you creep!"

The devil is just like that. He tries to force us to think junky, trashy, unproductive thoughts, and then he tries to get us to dwell on them. He wants to fill us with 'junk food' thoughts so we'll be unhealthy and unfit for doing God's work.

I've got good news for you. You can tell the devil to take a hike, and take his nasty thoughts with him! You have the authority of God on your side to resist even the worst thoughts.

When you are tempted with wrong thinking simply say to the devil "I resist you satan, you and your filthy thinking. Leave me alone! The blood of Jesus has cleansed my mind and he is changing my thought life to please him!" (Say it out loud to let the devil know he's defeated!)

Then go fill yourself up with the good food of the Word of God, allowing it to nourish you and clean out your mind. Focus on positive, godly, uplifting thoughts and the spirit of God will strengthen you and rush in to help you in this new discipline.

As your thoughts become positive and noble, your actions will follow. You will become a likeable and cheery person. Your life will be filled with joy instead of fear and doubt.

It is possible to change your mind. God will help you fill it with godly, sound thinking instead of trashy harmful thinking. All you have to do is co-operate with God, and He'll train you to develop a mind that He can use for His glory and for the use of His kingdom.

Don't give up. You have to discipline yourself to right thinking. One way to be sure you'll succeed is to block out any junk-media. (Computer, TV, radio, CD's . . . anything that pumps your brain full of trash.) Start fresh with Christian programming, and screen out the garbage that poisons your brain!

Don't be hard on yourself when you fail. They'll be times when you'll be disappointed with the thoughts you've allowed to run through your mind. Just be even more determined to let God renovate your brain, and you'll find out that His power will come to your rescue over and over again. Let God change you mind!

GET A BETTER GRIP by reading:
Philippians 4:8   Romans 8:5-11

What did God speak to me today through this chapter?

What action do I need to take in my life to apply what I have learned?

Chapter 12

The Ultimate Champion
(Jesus Christ the Resurrected King)
Colossians 1:22-23

"But now, by giving himself completely at the Cross, actually dying for you, Christ brought you over to God's side and put your lives together, whole and holy in his presence. <u>You don't walk away from a gift like that!</u> You stay grounded and steady in that bond of trust, constantly tuned in to the Message, careful not to be distracted or diverted. There is no other Message-just this one. Every creature under heaven gets this same Message. I Paul, am a messenger of this Message."

Professional athletes would love to be called the "Ultimate Champion" of their sport. Michael Jordan accomplished that feat! But, like any other human competitor, someday there will be a basketball star that will outshine Mike! In the world, no ultimate champion really exists.

There's only one Universal Champion, and He'll never lose his title! He's the ultimate extreme God-man. His name is Jesus Christ.

He endured the most extreme test any person has ever endured, and He triumphed!

Jesus Christ was falsely accused, tried and found guilty even though he was innocent. He was beaten until no one could recognize him, the flesh on his body hanging in strips. Then he was spiked to two crude wooden beams, hanging there suffering for nine hours.

His body bled profusely from the wounds. One inch thorns pierced his head. Even the effort to breathe caused excruciating pain.

Jesus hung there of his own free will, for it was his Father's plan that through His death and resurrection all mankind would have an opportunity to be brought back into a relationship with God.

He took <u>your</u> place, yours and mine. We were the ones guilty of sin and rebellion towards God. And even though Jesus knew he was innocent and we were guilty, He chose to take our place of punishment so we did not have to stand accused before God.

When His horrendous suffering was over, He died and was buried in the tomb of a rich man named Joseph. All his close friends were heartbroken.

On the third day, God delivered His triumphant Son! He supernaturally breathed power and life into Jesus' body, and He was raised from the dead to join God the father in heaven and to sit at God's place of honor as the victor and champion over sin, death and the grave!

His entire life was lived for this reason-that you might live as God's friend and not his enemy. As a Christian, you no longer stand accused of sin and doomed to hell. When God looks at you He sees you as holy and blameless because of Jesus.

You don't have to be ashamed anymore. Jesus carried the shame and heartache of your sin to the cross and swept them away forever in rivers of His own blood.

It is important to be secure and confident knowing that you have the hope of spending eternity in heaven with God. It is also vital to know that you must continue holding firmly to your new faith! Fight for it! Hold onto your new trust in God.

Jesus made a priceless sacrifice so you could be rescued from darkness; your life was ransomed away from the devil and the certain punishment of hell.

To live flippantly, immorally or impurely after accepting Christ's ultimate gift of a new life is a mockery. Ask for His help to escape from sinful lifestyle choices. The one who died to set you free from hell is powerfully able to set you free from sinful habits that are destroying you!

Jesus is faithful and able to strengthen you to live a life that is pleasing to Him. He will help you obey if you are willing.

God's son is the Extreme Ultimate Champion! No one in the universe, no human being or spirit being, has done what Jesus did. And he did it for YOU!

"You don't walk away from a gift like that!"

GET A BETTER GRIP by reading:
2 Corinthians 5:21   Galatians 3:13, 14

What did God speak to me today through this chapter?

What action do I need to take in my life to apply what I have learned?

Chapter 13

God Wants to Use You
(You have a ministry)
Colossians 1:24-29

"I want you to know how glad I am that it's me sitting here in this jail and not you. There's alot of suffering to be entered into in this world-the kind of suffering Christ takes on. I welcome the chance to take my share in the church's part of that suffering. When I became a servant in this church, I experienced this suffering as a sheer gift, God's way of helping me serve you, laying out the whole truth. This mystery has been kept in the dark for a long time, but now it's out in the open. God wanted everyone, not just Jews, to know this rich and glorious secret inside and out, regardless of their background, regardless of their religious standing. The mystery in a nutshell is just this: Christ is in you, therefore you can look forward to sharing in God's glory. It's that simple. That is the substance of our Message. We preach Christ, warning people not to add to the Message. We teach in a spirit of profound common sense so that we can bring each person to maturity. To be mature is to be basic. Christ! No more, no less. That's what I'm working so hard at day after day, year after year, doing my best with the energy God so generously gives me."

Paul was a wild-man. He was a sold out, on fire, pumped up man of God! Paul's job as an 'apostle' (a messenger selected by God to preach the gospel) was to tell people there was hope for their lives, hope for life on earth and hope for eternity. God gave him the privilege of teaching and preaching the entire truth about Christ's life, death and resurrection to those who would listen.

God placed a 'call' (commissioned) Paul to serve Him as a preacher/teacher. God brought about radical changes in Paul's life. He was formerly a religious leader who hated all Christians! He worked hard to see these Christians imprisoned and punished for their faith.

But when Paul had a dramatic encounter with God, it completely transformed him. He spent the rest of his life sharing the hope of faith in Jesus Christ. God used Paul to reach thousands of people who would never have heard that God loved them and would forgive their sin.

God has also determined to use you to reach others who are lost in their sin. Some of those may even be 'religious' like Paul! But if they do not know Jesus Christ as their personal Savior; they are still living in darkness, serving gods that are not really gods at all.

Don't be afraid to talk openly about what God had done for you! Nothing is more important than a person's spiritual condition. If you share the good news with a lost person, he or she will thank you on Judgment Day! Take every available opportunity to tell others what Christ has done in your life.

You may want to ask them a question like "Hey, have you planned ahead where you're going to spend eternity?" Or maybe you can simply do a good deed for them, smile, and say "I did this for you in the name of Jesus."

Witnessing (sharing your faith with the lost) is not complicated at all. God simply asks that you be available and willing to minister for Him at any opportunity. Just obey what you think the Holy Spirit is asking you to say or do, and then leave the rest in God's hands.

You really can't make a mistake when you share your faith. There are no 'professionals' who have witnessing down pat. Each person God sends your way is unique, each situation is different.

Just relax and share God's love and mercy.

You are a crucial asset to God's kingdom. He wants to pour His spirit on you so you can speak out about Him to those who will listen. Trust Him to do the work of penetrating people's hearts. Don't worry about the outcome of sharing your faith. You may never know what happens to the person you spoke with. Just trust God to sow a good seed in their heart, believing that in the right time that seed will bear fruit.

And don't feel bad if your message is rejected by some, or if you suffer insults from those who despise Jesus Christ. Don't take it personally! In fact, go ahead and react with joy, because Jesus said "You're <u>blessed</u> when your commitment to God provokes persecution. The persecution drives you even deeper into God's kingdom! (Matthew 5:10/The Message)

It's fine to invite people to your church, but it's even better to share the love of God with them right then and there, right where you are. God has not just appointed your pastor to talk to people about Christ. He has commanded <u>you</u> to 'let your light shine!'

And one more thing-don't make excuses like 'I'm afraid' or 'Let someone do it that has a more outgoing personality.' God wants to use YOU with all your weaknesses and problems. No, you're not perfect. Who is? He'll use you anyway!

GET A BETTER GRIP by reading:
2 Corinthians 5:20   Acts 8:26-38

What did God speak to me today through this chapter?

What action do I need to take in my life to apply what I have learned?

Chapter 14

Praying For Strangers
(Learning to be an intercessor)
Colossians 2:1

"I want you to realize that I continue to work as hard as I know how for you, and also for the Christians over at Laocidea. Not many of you have met me face to face, but that doesn't make any difference. Know that I'm on your side, right alongside you. You're not in this alone."

What if you found out that someone, somewhere in the world, was praying for you and you didn't even know it? It happens all the time! God may put a certain name, or the face of a person, or just a heavy burden on the heart of a believer, and will prompt the believer to pray for someone that he/she may not even know personally. How absolutely cool.

Perhaps the believer will never find out what those urgent prayers were all about. Then again, God may choose to reveal the results of those prayers at some future appointed time.

It's not really important if we discover what has happened because we have prayed. What is important is that we obey the Holy Spirit's nudging, and pray!

Prayer is a forceful and formidable power. It is mighty enough to bring about the will of God in situations that seem impossible.

At times God will stir your heart to pray for someone you have seen on T.V., someone you have passed in the grocery store, or a person you've read about in the news. That is God's way of helping that person. It's not crazy or whacko, you are just responding to God's nudging!

He knows what kind of circumstance that person is in, and He wants believers like you to be willing to pray even when you don't personally know the one you are praying for.

For example, when I read about a certain actress having serious personal problems, I began to pray for her even though I had never met her. The Lord stirred my heart to pray some specific things that I could not have known except through the Holy Spirit's leading. Some years later I discovered that she had become a Christian. Perhaps my prayers contributed to her coming to know Christ. I'm believing they did!

Would you be willing to pray for a complete stranger? Can God count on you to join an army of 'intercessors' (people who pray diligently for people and situations) so that His will can be accomplished?

The apostle Paul said in this verse that he was praying for those he had not met personally. He was willing to allow the Lord to use him in this work of prayer. And it <u>can</u> be <u>work</u> praying for strangers. Because you don't know them, it's easy to let your mind wander and to forget to keep praying. However, God will help you and train you to keep working at it, because He wants every person on the face of the earth to come to know Him as Savior.

Although you may never know who, I'll bet that God had some-one praying for you before you gave your heart to Jesus. Perhaps you will meet them in heaven, or maybe God will arrange a meeting on earth. In any case, God wants to recruit you to be a 'power pray-er' for His kingdom.

All you have to do is be willing and tell the Lord, "Lord, start using me to pray for people all over the world!" I promise you, He'll do just that.

GET A BETTER GRIP by reading:
John 17:20-21   I Timothy 2:1

What did God speak to me today through this chapter?

What action do I need to take in my life to apply what I have learned?

Chapter 15

Jesus Christ Is Enough
(Jesus: The only road to heaven)
Colossians 2:2-5

"I want you woven into a tapestry of love, in touch with every-thing there is to know of God. Then you will have minds confi-dent and at rest, focused on Christ, God's great mystery. All the richest treasures of wisdom and knowledge are embedded in that mystery and nowhere else. And we've been shown the mystery! I'm telling you this because I don't want anyone lead-ing you off on some wild-goose chase, after other so-called mysteries or 'the Secret.' I'm a long way off, true, and you may never lay eyes on me, but believe me, I'm on your side, right beside you. I am delighted to hear of the careful and orderly ways you conduct your affairs, and impressed with the solid substance of your faith in Christ."

Have you ever gotten discouraged about not having enough money? Enough time? Enough energy to finish a job? Does it sometimes seem as if you are always lacking something? Everyone seems to struggle with those feelings.

There is one area of your life where you will never have to be concerned about having enough. When Jesus Christ suffered and died for you His death was <u>enough </u>to pay for your sins once and for all. You will never have to worry about having enough good works to get into heaven, because it isn't your good deeds that win you a place in heaven, it's Christ's death and resurrection and your faith in Him that get you into heaven!

There are a lot of scary 'religious' philosophies being passed around these days. Some of those philosophies claim that there are many ways to get to God. They deny that Jesus is the one and only road to heaven. These philosophies are really only empty teachings and interesting sounding arguments. Their main goal is to distract people from the truth of the good news that you can know God personally through Jesus Christ His Son.

Other false teachings try to claim that Jesus wasn't really God, He was simply a good man like Muhammad or Gandhi, that Jesus' sacrifice on the cross cannot save anyone, that His resurrection never took place, and that we must run after other mystical experiences to 'spiritually connect' with God.

Many cults attempt to convince people that the way to be saved is by completing a list of 'good works' or by following a man or woman who claim their teachings are to be obeyed above the Bible. Be on guard against any philosophy or teaching that tries to sell these ideas to you. It is a dangerous thing to become involved with groups that peddle worthless notions like these.

In fact, the Bible has some strong words about this issue: "The Spirit makes it clear that as time goes on, some are going to give up on the faith and chase after demonic illusions put forth by professional liars. These liars have lied so well and for so long that they've lost their capacity for truth." (I Timothy 4:1-2)

Don't fool around by listening to clever sounding philosophies, even if they are cloaked in 'religious' terminology. There has never been, nor will there ever be, a human being who can add to or subtract from the plan of God for people to be saved by the way of Jesus Christ's death and powerful resurrection.

The truth is, Jesus Christ is enough, more than enough, to wash away your sin forever! If anyone tries to tell you differently, simply quote them this verse from God's powerful Word:

"He wants not only us but everyone saved, you know, everyone to get to know the truth we've learned: that there's one God and only one, and one Priest-Mediator between God and us – Jesus, who offered himself in exchange for everyone held captive by sin, to set them all free. Eventually the news is going to get out." (I Timothy 2:5-6)

GET A BETTER GRIP by reading:
Hebrews 10:11-14   I Timothy 1:6-7   2 Peter 3:17-18   Acts 4:12

What did God speak to me today through this chapter?

What action do I need to take in my life to apply what I have learned?

Chapter 16

Avoid False 'Spiritual' Teachers
Colossians 2:4-5

"And we've been shown the mystery! I'm telling you this because I don't want anyone leading you off on some wild-goose chase, after other so-called mysteries, or "the Secret." I'm a long way off, true, and you may never lay eyes on me, but believe me, I'm on your side, right beside you. I am delighted to hear of the careful and orderly ways you conduct your affairs, and impressed with the solid substance of your faith in Christ."

If you are hungering after a close relationship with God, you are a threat to your enemy the devil (satan). He will try to do everything he can to distract you from pursuing intimacy with Jesus. Because he is the 'deceiver' and the 'father of lies' (John 8:44) he may plant false spiritual teachers in your way, hoping to fool you into falling for their lies.

These men and women may be attractive, kind, and seem very helpful and interested in your life, but they will not teach you the truth, nor will they live a life that meets biblical standards for holiness and integrity.

These people are dangerous because they may cloak themselves in scripture and spiritual sounding literature in their attempts to fool you, so it will seem like they are speaking and teaching the truth. However, if you ask God for a discerning heart He will show you their errors and will uncover their sin.

How can you tell the difference between a false teacher and a man or woman of God who is faithfully teaching or preaching God's Word? Here are some guidelines to follow to recognize a false teacher:

- They will focus on a varied number of subjects instead of Jesus Christ, repenting of sins, living a holy life and serving God in humility.
- They will boast about spiritual visions, dreams and other supernatural revelations they have had, puffing themselves up to look important, unique and especially gifted by these 'mystical experiences.' They'll try to pass these experiences off as 'divine' and 'from God.'
- They like to produce 'new thinking' which they say surpasses the authority of the Bible; they consider Jesus Christ as just a 'starting place' for spiritual things, instead of the end-all answer.
- They like to be the center of attention, often controlling those around them.
- Their ministry will be built on money, fame, personality, and popularity.
- They will attempt to seem humble, but when pressed will show their true colors, their pride.
- Their teachings will include self-made, (or twisted truth) rules and promises of heaven if you live by 'their' rules.
- Almost always they will be living a life of sexual immorality.
- They will twist and warp the meaning of scripture to fit their opinions and lifestyle choices.
- The people who follow them faithfully are blinded by deceit and emptiness, rendering them helpless against sin. They will be encouraged to isolate themselves from Bible-believing Christians.

God will not allow you to be led astray by false teachers if you continue to read His Word, stay connected to Him through prayer, and stay clean by repenting of your sins on a daily basis. Jesus Christ knows how to keep and sustain you and train you to recognize falsehood when you hear it, standing firm in your faith in God. Ask Him for His wisdom and His discernment so you can live and walk in the truth of God's Word.

No one likes to be lied to. If you've been drawn into a group like the ones I have described above, <u>get out now</u>. Get help from a Word-based Church or ministry (they believe the Bible is the inspired, unfailing Word of God and that Jesus is the only Savior and Messiah). Don't wait to 'challenge' the group leaders with your newfound understanding. Leave immediately and don't leave a forwarding address!

GET A BETTER GRIP by reading:
I John 2:22-23   2 Peter 3:17   Matthew 24:23-26   Titus 1:11

What did God speak to me today through this chapter?

What action do I need to take in my life to apply what I have learned?

Chapter 17

You've Got to Have Roots
(How to succeed as a Christian)
Colossians 2:6-7

". . . just go ahead with what you've been given. You received Christ Jesus, the Master; now live him. You're deeply rooted in him. You're well constructed upon him. You know your way around the faith. Now do what you've been taught. School's out; quit studying the subject and start living it! And let your living spill over into thanksgiving."

When an oak tree puts down deep roots it is almost immovable. The roots snake their way underground, anchoring the tree so firmly in the soil that though many storms batter the tree above ground it refuses to budge from its place. Talk about strong!

Do you want to be an incredible, rugged believer? You can be! In order to stand strong and immovable in your new life with Christ you must send some deep roots into Jesus.

When you accepted Christ as your savior, You probably intended to serve Him for the rest of your life. Most people do, but when hard times come along, some quickly fall away if they have not determined to root themselves in the truths of God. You can't be a wimp in the kingdom of God! It takes guts, courage and mental toughness to grip the things of God, especially when trouble or persecution comes.

How can you thrust your roots deeply into Jesus? Here are 3 ways:

1. **Obey His instructions in His Word, the Bible, every day:** The Bible is the only absolute truth existing. Instructions from the Lord keep you safe, allow you to live life abundantly, and generate wholeness and completeness when you follow them. Obedient living is a sure way to bring your life into focus, to manage your gifts and abilities, and to find sincere fulfillment. Many people say they are believers, and they may go to church, pay tithes (you'll learn about tithes in Chapter 23) and hang out with other Christians. But if they are deliberately living in some sort of continual rebellion to what God's Word teaches they are walking in disobedience to God. The Bible says: "If someone claims 'I know Him well!' but doesn't keep his commandments, he's obviously a liar. His life doesn't match his words. But the one who keeps God's word is the person in whom we see God's mature love. This is the only way to be sure we're in God." (I John 2:4)

2. **Absorb God's Word through music, teachings, and reading:** Hang out with believing friends, listen to worship music. Go hear an awesome, bible believing pastor preach. Buy teaching and preaching tapes from experienced, godly men and women. Go to classes that teach you about Christian living. Read your Bible everyday, not just once in awhile. Be a sponge!

3. **Get up in the morning, shout "THANK YOU LORD!" and keep thanking Him all day long:** There is supernatural, devil-blitzing power in thanks-giving! When you hold a cup under a running faucet, it overflows. And because God has drenched your life in blessings, you should express your gratitude to Him through overflowing praise, worship,

singing and rejoicing. Lifting your hands, clapping, shouting for joy, singing, dancing and rejoicing are all wonderful expressions of thankfulness!

When your circumstances are difficult and look hopeless, take extra time to thank God. All things come from His hand, both hard times and good times, and He has instructed us to give thanks to Him!

Something astonishing begins to happen when you give thanks in hard situations. The circumstances may look the same, but incredible joy starts rising from deep inside your chest. If you keep giving thanks, you'll feel like you're going to explode with joy!

That's proof that the Spirit of God is saying "I'll work this out! You'll see! Just watch my mighty hand do powerful things for you!"

Enjoy your life. Don't let the devil steal your time and joy any longer. God doesn't want you to be blown, tossed and stripped by every storm that comes along. He wants you to live your life to the fullest by deepening your relationship with Him. You will find that you can endure anything if your faith is strong, firm and anchored in Christ.

GET A BETTER GRIP by reading:
Philippians 4:4 I   Thessalonians 5:16-18   I John 5:2-5
Psalm 1:1-3

What did God speak to me today through this chapter?

What action do I need to take in my life to apply what I have learned?

Chapter 18

Empty, Worldly Philosophies
Colossians 2:8

"Watch out for people who try to dazzle you with big words and intellectual double-talk. They want to drag you off into endless arguments that never amount to anything. They spread their ideas through the empty traditions of human beings and the empty superstitions of spirit beings. But that's not the way of Christ."

We've all heard the tall tale. Humans evolved from wiggly, mud sucking goop-slime into intelligent, gifted beings who are able to deliver a discourse on the molecular structure of Jupiter, can split the atom, and can throw a party for their parent's 30th anniversary. *P-lease!* Spare me the high-minded double talk! That scientifically unproven philosophy is simply a cover-up for choosing to reject God.

God created humans with an eternal soul, and each individual was created for a specific, divine purpose. We have not evolved; we were created by a personal and loving God.

Today's world is filled with empty philosophies that de-value human life and attempt to explain away God's presence and plan for His creation. Evolution, communism, new age ideas, wicca, abortion, euthanasia, and secular humanism are all assaults against the authority and wisdom of God. People who choose to believe those philosophies are really choosing to reject God!

The common thread that runs through these hollow ideas is the contempt for holiness and God's absolute standard of right and wrong. Most folks who embrace these radical ideologies are looking for a way to gain personal power, unrestricted sexual encounters, money, or prestige.

Empty philosophies fill our world with empty people, people without hope and purpose. If you have been taught some of these ideas, it should make you angry that you have been duped! They've lied to you! And they're not apologizing.

None of these philosophies will lead you to truth and to an eternity with God, your creator. When an idea is not rooted in God's Word, it is an idea doomed to failure.

The basic principles of this world can be scientifically intriguing, but they cannot explain what makes a human spirit long for a relationship with God. Human tradition can give someone a temporary sense of security, but it cannot reveal truth. When we look for fulfillment outside of God, we look in vain, for all other avenues are dead ends.

If your mind has been steeped in these ideas, you need to break free through the power of the Holy Spirit. He alone has the ability to show you truth in a way that convinces you.

Ask Him today to set you free from a 'worldly mindset.' If you are in a profession where these ideas are accepted and practiced, you will need to ask the Lord to renew your mind in His Word and fill you with His truth.

He will give you wisdom to be able to refute those who refuse to believe God's truth, and power to stand firm in the truth you have been shown. The Bible promises you that "others . . . went up against him trying to argue him down. But they were no match for his wisdom and spirit when he spoke." (Acts 6:10/The Message)

God will fill you with revelations, understanding and insight to counter every argument and opposition to the truth. Don't be afraid to speak up! When you do, God will protect you like He protected Jesus when the townspeople wanted to stone him, yet he walked right past them and escaped.

GET A BETTER GRIP by reading:
Philippians 1:27-30   Galatians 4:3-6   I Timothy 6:20

What did God speak to me today through this chapter?

What action do I need to take in my life to apply what I have learned?

Chapter 19

God the Father, God the Son, God the Holy Spirit
(The Trinity)
Colossians 2:9-10

"Everything of God gets expressed in him, so you can see and hear him clearly. You don't need a telescope, a microscope, or a horoscope to realize the fullness of Christ, and the emptiness of the universe without him. When you come to him, that fullness comes together for you, too. His power extends over everything."

You are FULL of Him! Yes, if you have Jesus Christ the Son living in you, then you also have God the Father and God the Holy Spirit living in you too! All together they are called the TRINITY. These three spirit beings have three different personalities but are ONE GOD.

A simple example of this is an egg. One egg has three parts: the shell, the white and the yoke, but it is only <u>one</u> egg. Even though you call each part a different name and each have different appearances, you still recognize that it is only <u>one</u> egg.

You are FILLED to the brim with the presence of God if you have accepted Jesus Christ as your Savior. You need not fear the anger of the Father, because Jesus made peace between you two by his death on the cross. Don't fear being rejected by the Son, for He loved you when you were still living in sin. Don't tremble at the thought of the Holy Spirit, He has come to teach you all truth, comfort you, strengthen you, and empower you.

You may wonder to which of these three you pray! The answer is all three. When you pray, the Holy Spirit helps you pray, Jesus Christ hears your prayers, and with compassion intercedes with the Father for your needs, and God the Father according to His will favors you with an answer.

Jesus Christ is the only one of the three that took upon Himself a human body so that He might participate in our weaknesses. The Father and the Holy Spirit have always been 'Spirits' and are invisible to our human eyes. But God promises that someday we shall see Him in all of His power and glory, and we will be awestruck.

Some world religions worship many gods. The God of the Bible is only ONE God that shows Himself in three forms. Those who worship gods other than the One True God are worshipping in vain. These gods are idols and imaginations, statues of stone or simple men with no power to save, heal or deliver from sin and hell.

When the high priest asked Jesus whether He was the son of God, Jesus answered,

"You yourself said it. And that's not all. Soon you'll see it for yourself: the Son of Man seated at the right hand of the Mighty One, arriving on the clouds of heaven." (Matthew 26:64, New International Version)

Jesus was not a liar, nor was he a crazy man. He was the true son of God.

The word Trinity is not in the Bible, but you will find many scriptures that reveal the three-part nature of God (including those listed below). Even when we think we understand Him, there is so much more to discover about who He is and what He wants to do in our lives.

GET A BETTER GRIP by reading:
Romans 1:1-4   John 3:34-36

What did God speak to me today through this chapter?

What action do I need to take in my life to apply what I have learned?

Chapter 20

The Supernatural Super Soaker
(Water Baptism)

Colossians 2:12

"If it's an initiation ritual you're after, you've already been
through it by submitting to baptism. Going under the water was
a burial of your old life; coming up out of it was a resurrection,
God raising you from the dead as he did Christ."

Has anyone told you that after you accept Jesus as your Savior,
you need to be water baptized? Well now you know, so go
call your pastor and set up a time to do it!

Don't do things just because it's a cool tradition. Jesus told us to
be baptized, and to prove how serious He was about it He himself
was baptized to be an example for us, even though he had never
sinned and didn't need God's forgiveness.

He laid down a pattern for believers to follow in order to please
God and fulfill His commands.

When you are baptized in water, it represents Jesus washing
your sins away, raising you up as a new person, and burying your
old, sinful lifestyle.

It's a Supernatural Super Soaker! When you come up out of that
water, I imagine the angels high-fiving and the Father boasting
about you to the saints in heaven. Every Christian at your baptism

will be celebrating with you!

You may be baptized at church, in a pool or in a lake. It isn't the place that is important, only your sincere heart. When you have denounced your life of sin, asked Jesus for forgiveness, and decided to live for Christ, it's time to be baptized.

Many people are baptized as babies and want to know if that applies to the command to be water baptized. When you were an infant it would have been impossible to make a personal choice to serve God, so your 'infant baptism' was more like a 'dedication.' Thank God your parents made the wise choice to dedicate you to Christ! However, that was not the baptism of a new believer.

Now that you are aware of His requirements and have chosen to make Him the Lord of your life, you must be baptized as a sign of your choice to serve God wholeheartedly.

Remember, water baptism does not save you. It is Jesus Christ, his death and resurrection and your faith in Him that saves you.

When you are baptized you are publicly confessing your belief in Christ as the living Son of God, your Savior, whom you will serve until your death. You don't have to wear certain clothing or be any special place to be baptized. God, who sees your heart, will honor your water baptism as a sign of your identification and obedience to Jesus as your Lord.

So, what are you waiting for? Now's the time! God has sent you an invitation to be 'Super Soaked,' proclaiming to all the world that you've been supernaturally saved!

GET A BETTER GRIP by reading:
I Peter 3:21   Acts 8:12   Acts 8:36-38

What did God speak to me today through this chapter?

What action do I need to take in my life to apply what I have learned?

Chapter 21

Cancel That Date With Death!
(You will live forever!)
Colossians 2:13-14

"When you were stuck in your old sin-dead life, you were incapable of responding to God. God brought you alive-right along with Christ! Think of it! All sins forgiven, the slate wiped clean, that old arrest warrant canceled and nailed to Christ's Cross."

Death runs in my family, how about yours? The latest statistics prove that 1 out of every 1 person will die in a lifetime! Just like physical death is inescapable, spiritual death (hell) is inescapable unless you cancel that date with death.

At one time you were like the walking dead, a zombie. You were unable to respond to spiritual things, incapable of understanding the Bible, unable to grasp moral concepts. You were helpless and weak against the power of sin! You had a huge sin debt piled up, and you couldn't pay.

You had a date with DEATH . . . because anyone living in sin is living in spiritual death, continually piling up sins until the moment of death, when the spirit leaves the body and is separated from God for eternity.

God saw that you were unable to afford the high price required to pay back your sin debt, so he sent his priceless son Jesus to die, nailing your debt to His cross and canceling ALL of the sin in your life.

There are two awesome details here:

1. That God Almighty, the maker of the universe, would have so much mercy on someone living in sin and rebellion.

2. That ABSOLUTELY ALL of your sins were paid in full through Jesus' personal sacrifice!

You never have to be afraid that God will bring up your past sins and punish you for them. The Bible says that God puts your sin out of sight, out of reach, out of mind, and out of existence. (Micah 7:19, Psalm 103:12, Jeremiah 31:34, Isaiah 43:25)

As for the sins you may commit today, you need to ask for His forgiveness when you sin, and then live in repentance (which means you turn from those sins and won't willfully commit them anymore). He knows you are not perfect, and that you will make many, many mistakes, so don't live in self-condemnation.

But also realize that you cannot continually practice willfully sinning, because your conscience will become deadened and your life in Christ will be jeopardized.

When you have Jesus Christ in your life, your date with eternal death is canceled! You don't have to fear dying ever again. When you die with Christ in your heart, you can be certain that heaven will be your eternal home. That's the reason Christians live in peace! We are assured that whenever death comes, we are not 'losing' our life but we are gaining life eternal.

GET A BETTER GRIP by reading:
John 5:24   I John 1:8-10   Hebrews 10:26-27

What did God speak to me today through this chapter?

What action do I need to take in my life to apply what I have learned?

Chapter 22

The Fallen Angel Called Satan
Colossians 2:15

"He stripped all the spiritual tyrants in the universe of their sham authority at the Cross and marched them naked through the streets."

I f you're expecting to read about a man-like creature with red horns and a tail holding a pitchfork you're reading the wrong book! That's a fairy-tale version of the very real, very active evil one.

Satan is a spirit-being, not a human being, and he certainly is not a 'god.' He isn't all-wise and he cannot be everywhere at once like THE God. He is known by many names: the devil, Lucifer, satan, the destroyer. But he is real, just as real as God.

He was originally created by God and was a beautiful angel, full of wisdom and anointed by God. The name 'Lucifer' means 'Light Bearer.' Apparently God originally intended this mighty angel to carry His light and goodness to all parts of His creation. But because of satan's excellence and splendor, his heart became proud and he was filled with wickedness.

The devil wanted to take God's place as supreme master and ruler of the universe, so he recruited one-third of the angels of heaven to rebel against God in an attempt to conquer heaven. The Bible records that God flung him to earth with all his rebellious followers, and they became known as fallen angels (demons).

These demons, led by their rebellious leader satan, roam throughout the earth and the skies, filling the earth with violence and hatred. They use people and circumstances to further their cause.

Anyone practicing witchcraft, occultic games, addicted to drugs, dealing drugs, or who messes with black magic fantasy books, games or videos is an open target for satan, allowing themselves to be deceived, and will eventually be oppressed or possessed by demons.

The devil and his evil angels do all they can to try to lead people into damaging and sinful lifestyles so they can capture their souls for eternity. In the beginning, they make a sinful lifestyle look enticing, fun and filled with adventure. But once you are entangled in their web the downward spiral begins. You will lose your health, your mind, your finances, and your peace. They will stop at nothing to make certain you are destroyed. They don't want to be in hell alone! They hate Almighty God so much, their desire is to destroy God's most favored creation: people. That's you and that's me.

It is almost hard to imagine that someone or something could be so utterly evil, until you remember men like Adolf Hitler. At some point in his life, Adolf Hitler allowed the devil to take control of him. The result was the holocaust, the murder of over 6 million Jewish people, and millions of other men, women and children.

The devil has a twisted, hateful and vengeful mind toward all human beings, because we were created in the image of the God he despises. Never doubt for a moment the depth of his hatred towards you.

Until the moment Jesus died on the cross, satan had ruler-ship on the earth, given to him through the sin and disobedience of Adam and Eve. When Jesus breathed his last, the power of the devil, sin and death were broken, granting the people of the earth freedom, but only through faith in Christ. Those who do not believe are still under the rule and authority of satan. Jesus stripped the devil and his demons of their authority to rule all those who would believe in His name, Jesus, the only Son of God.

Satan will still work to deceive you, to lie to you, to tempt you and to discourage you, but he has no real power over you if you have confessed Jesus as Lord and Savior of your life.

When you sense a spiritual attack from the devil coming against you, simply use the name of JESUS (which has been given to you for your protection), quote scripture, (which are the words of God that contain power to fight back) and resist the attack by asking God for his help and grace.

Remember, Jesus DIED to give you overcoming power, so it is available to you anytime, anywhere. Memorize the words of God found in the Bible, and use them liberally. Print them up on sticky notes and place them all over your house to remind you of God's truths. They are amazingly full of supernatural power, unlike our own words.

When you use God's truths found in the Bible to fight the enemy of your soul, he must run away from you. That is a promise! And God will never let you be tempted beyond what you can bear, but He will make a way of escape for you so you can stand up under that evil temptation.

Trust God to help you during difficult moments in your life, and don't waste time worrying and fretting. Memorize God's Word, which tells you what God's plans are for you!

It is important to know the devil is your enemy and is trying to lead you away from God in any way he can. However, don't spend your time focusing on that. Spend your time drawing near to God and talking about God. Focus on His awesome, overcoming power. Confess that His keeping power is equal to His saving power!

You needn't fear the devil. He is like a toothless lion in your life. Reverence God and be awestruck by God, and let Him take care of the devil, that evil fallen angel.

GET A BETTER GRIP by reading:
James 4:7-8   Luke 10:18-20   Hebrews 4:12   Ephesians 6:10-18
I John 5:18

What did God speak to me today through this chapter?

What action do I need to take in my life to apply what I have learned?

Chapter 23

You Can't Get to Heaven Through Man-Made Rules
Colossians 2:16-17

"So don't put up with anyone pressuring you in details of diet, worship services, or holy days. All those things are mere shadows cast before what was to come; the substance is Christ."

A shadow is just a hazy image of the real thing. Shadows aren't reality. Some people still believe that in order to please God or to be 'religious' they must follow a certain set of rules or ideas that are man-made.

Those rules are like shadows. If you reached out to touch them you would find only emptiness.

Perhaps you have been taught that attending church a certain number of times, or giving money, or practicing a certain set of requirements will get you into heaven. The Bible, however, clearly teaches that these things cannot win you a place in heaven or give you eternal life with Christ.

When Jesus Christ came to earth He declared:

"I am the way, the truth, and the life. No man comes to the Father except through me."

Only by repenting of your sins and believing in Jesus Christ can you be made right in the sight of God. Then He has promised to take you to heaven when you die.

Abiding by a set of 'do's and 'do not's' is not real Christianity. Giving money and going to church are wonderful and praiseworthy deeds, but those deeds cannot save you. Loving Jesus and obeying his commands is what really pleases God and brings you salvation and the hope of heaven.

It is right to be in God's house to worship Him regularly, and it is important to obey God by giving 10% of your income (called a TITHE) to your local church to do the work of the ministry. But if you are counting on those things to reserve for you a place in heaven you are terribly mistaken.

God asks you to love and obey His Son, to live a holy life by avoiding sin and the things that would cause you to sin, and to respond with His compassion to all people. But rules and regulations (like only eating certain things, or celebrating certain ceremonies, or punishing your body, or bowing to a man, an idol or a place) have no power to save you from your sins.

Many people will go to their grave thinking that they have guaranteed themselves a place in heaven by doing good works or attending a 'religious' house. The devil would like nothing better than to fool people in this way. It is only through Jesus Christ that people can be saved.

Once you have accepted Jesus as Lord and Savior, it is vital for you to serve Him by doing what He has called you to do. Feed the poor, love your neighbor, share Christ freely and openly, and give generously to God's work. Build up the kingdom of God on earth, and He will be pleased. It is important to make sure you spread the news that good deeds alone can never get a person to heaven.

GET A BETTER GRIP by reading:
John 3:16   Ephesians 2:9-10   I John 5:11-12

What did God speak to me today through this chapter?

What action do I need to take in my life to apply what I have learned?

Chapter 24

"UFO's: God's Powerful Angels"
Colossians 2:18-19

"Don't tolerate people who try to run your life, ordering you to bow and scrape, insisting that you join their obsession with angels and that you seek out visions. They're a lot of hot air, that's all they are. They're completely out of touch with the source of life, Christ, who puts us together in one piece, whose very breath and blood flow through us. He is the Head and we are the body. We can grow up healthy in God only as he nourishes us."

True story: A 19 year old college freshman fell from a bridge, was knocked unconscious and was drowning, yet the next thing he knew he awoke standing on the river bank.

True story: An elderly lady was traveling down a 4 lane highway and saw a car in her lane headed straight towards her! She cried 'Jesus!' and instantly found herself on the other side of the median, traveling the opposite way, safely distanced from the erratic driver.

Both stories happened to people I know personally. These two Christians experienced the intervention of God in their emergencies, most likely through angelic beings. Other people have shared stories of encountering those they thought were 'people' helping them in dire circumstances, only to discover these 'people' could not be accounted for afterwards!

Holy angels are real, and they really do intervene to help people according to God's will. They are incredible beings! The Bible records that they are large, shining beings who strike awe in the hearts of those who see them. God created them, and He commissions them to fulfill certain tasks. They are God's helpers, and they are loyal only to Him.

Some angels stand before the great throne of God and offer glory, honor and praise to the Most High. Others are sent to minister to human beings by protecting us and providing unseen guidance and help. Some angels are sent to give people messages from God. They are supernatural, and exercise supernatural powers under the authority of God Almighty and Jesus Christ His Son.

Angels are not male and female, but are gender neutral. They don't look like little cupids, with bows and arrows and cute chubby faces. Their role is serving God in worship and work, obeying His will and carrying out His commands.

They do not have a separate life of their own, and they have not fallen into sin like satan's demons (former angels). Their entire purpose is to honor God and further His work in the universe.

People in today's world are hungry for the supernatural. They have experienced the disappointments and hurts of life and they are looking for something outside of themselves to provide power, excitement and diversion. In their search for the supernatural, some people have become absorbed in "angel worship."

They are entranced by accounts of angels intervening in the lives of humans, and they begin to unwisely turn their eyes from God, who created the angels, and they exalt angels and other heavenly beings as if they were God.

This passage in Colossians says these kinds of people go into great detail about what they have seen. They are convinced that these mystical experiences somehow take the place of God's Word and seeking Christ for supernatural power. However, the truth is that God commands us in Matthew 4:10 "You shall worship the Lord your God, and serve Him only."

Scripture also says that people who fall into exalting angels and other supernatural beings have "lost connection with the HEAD," which is Christ.

That means that some who profess to be Christians will be drawn into these kinds of experiences because of their desire to see supernatural power at work. It is a normal part of the Christian life to want to witness God's power at work, and we should all be praying to witness His miracles, signs and wonders. But it is wrong to promote created beings over their creator, and you would be taking the wrong path by seeking 'power' experiences through angels.

Besides, you will experience the 'dark side' of the spiritual realm in your quest to get in touch with spirit beings. (Refer to chapter #22) Dabbling in horoscopes, psychic hot lines, or using a 'medium' to get in touch with a dead person are all dangerous forms of communication with the spirit world. Demonic powers operating in all forms of deception use those avenues to enter your life. Stay away from those things! God's spirit is against those who practice any form of the occult. (Read Isaiah 47:8-15; Revelation 21:8)

I Timothy 2:5 says there is only ONE GOD and only ONE mediator between God and man, and that is the man Christ Jesus. If you seek Him, He will provide you with all the powerful supernatural experiences you need.

Angels are to be respected as God's servants, messengers and helpers. But the focus of your Christian life should always be honoring and worshipping God as the creator of both humans and angels!

GET A BETTER GRIP by reading:
Hebrews 1:4-9 and 14   2 Corinthians 11:13-15   2 Peter 2:4
Psalm 91:11   Acts 12:7

What did God speak to me today through this scripture?

What action do I need to take in my life to apply what I have learned?

Chapter 25

Don't Punish Yourself
('Religious' self punishment doesn't please God)
Colossians 2:20-23

"So, then, if with Christ you've put all that pretentious and infantile religion behind you, why do you let yourselves be bullied by it? "Don't touch this! Don't taste that! Don't go near this!" Do you think things that are here today and gone tomorrow are worth that kind of attention? Such things sound impressive if said in a deep enough voice. They even give the illusion of being pious and humble and ascetic. But they're just another way of showing off, making yourselves look important."

There are religions all over the world that teach people many forms of self-punishment as a way to please God. These well meaning but terribly misguided folks are trying to find a way to get to God through abusing themselves, as if to say "We know we are not good enough to approach you God, and we know you can't be pleased with us."

These teachings make God out to be a sadistic and hostile being, who takes pleasure in humans hurting themselves or others. Nothing could be more wrong! Submitting to these sufferings doesn't make God happy and doesn't win any "points" with Him!

This scripture reveals that "religious" practices that demand harsh treatment of the body are based on human commands and teachings, and they appear to be wise but they only do harm.

Besides that, these 'self-punishments' cannot give you any power to keep from sinning. They are man-made regulations, and they won't help you find God or live a holy life.

God calls all these things "pretentious and infantile religion." And since you were saved, you don't belong anymore to the world system and its beliefs and its false religions. You are a new person! You are no longer required to live according to those self-punishing rules. You are free in Christ!

He has made you acceptable to God, because every time God looks at you He sees the blood and sacrifice of His son, and the Bible says that the Father is "well pleased" with the Son.

You do not have to fear that God is angry with you! He loved you so much He sacrificed His only Son to make certain you would live with Him forever in heaven.

God doesn't want you to live in continual guilt and self-condemnation, always feeling worthless and 'less-than.' The devil heaps those feelings and fears upon you. Don't believe those lies. You don't have to live in guilt over your sin anymore. Christ has taken your sin and your guilt and shame upon Himself once and for all.

So you can relax. Live your life by obeying God's commands as revealed in His Word and enjoy your new freedom, being certain and confident that God loves you and accepts you.

GET A BETTER GRIP by reading:
I Kings 18:16-39   I Timothy 4:1-4

What did God speak to me today through this chapter?

What action do I need to take in my life to apply what I have learned?

Chapter 26

The Ultimate Make-Over
(New mind, new mouth)
Colossians 3:1-4

"So if you're serious about living this new resurrection life with Christ, act like it. Pursue the things over which Christ presides. Don't shuffle along, eyes to the ground, absorbed with the things right in front of you. Look up, and be alert to what is going on around Christ—that's where the action is. See things from his perspective. Your old life is dead. Your new life, which is your real life—even though invisible to spectators, is with Christ in God. He is your life. When Christ (your real life, remember) shows up again on this earth, you'll show up, too—the real you, the glorious you. Meanwhile, be content with obscurity, like Christ."

What do you spend most of your time thinking about? Is your mind filled with negative and tormenting thoughts? Do you feel oppressed or depressed? Are the words that come out of your mouth critical, hateful, and filled with sourness and bitterness? Then you need a MIND and MOUTH MAKE-OVER!

Jesus Christ wants to totally rehabilitate, overhaul and re-condition your mind and mouth so you can live a life that is free from all of the bondages listed above.

Your spiritual enemy, the devil, wants you to live a defeated life, so he works very hard to try to keep your mind in the gutter. He knows if you begin experiencing freedom in your mind, the rest of you will follow.

His trick is to call your attention to something negative, then your flesh (the OLD you) starts to spit out nasty thoughts about the situation. Very soon those nasty thoughts become nasty words!

The devil wants to railroad you into believing that you don't have a choice about what goes into your mind and what you dwell on and think about. YOU DO HAVE A CHOICE! Every day you have the choice to take in trash that the devil throws at you and accept it, or to say 'NO devil, I will not think about the things you are trying to put in my mind! My mind is cleansed by the blood of Jesus Christ and my thought life is NEW!

I reject negative and critical thinking. I reject dirty and lustful thoughts; I reject the awful pictures you want me to think about. My mind is set on NEW THINGS . . . now I CHOOSE to think clean and wholesome thoughts. Every day I choose to focus on goodness and think thoughts that please God. I will dwell on and rehearse thoughts that bring me peace and joy and contentment. I will choose to think thoughts about other people that are positive and pure. I <u>will</u> fight this battle of choices, and I will win!

Poisoned thinking leads to poisoned words. If you choose to allow polluted thoughts to junk up your mind, eventually they will make their way to your mouth and escape. Those poisoned words destroy relationships and bring strife and division to families and friends.

Poisoned thinking also leads to depression. If you have wrestled with black, even suicidal thoughts, chances are your thought life has a great deal to do with it. When you lose hope, your thoughts become cynical, gloomy and pessimistic. If you wallow too long in those thoughts, they will swallow you up.

Your circumstances may be very difficult, but God wants to rescue you from depression. You must co-operate with the Holy Spirit by turning your thought life around.

Refuse to dwell on and mull over all your unfortunate circumstances. Begin looking for the positive in everything. Start looking for the hand of God operating in your situation; even if that means recognizing that He is using difficult things to correct your life! He's correcting you to change the course of your life for the better. That *is* a positive, even if it's painful.

So start with a MIND MAKE-OVER and I guarantee your MOUTH will follow!

Jesus promises He will give you constant supernatural power and strength to make the right thought choices. And when you fail, as we all do, He will forgive you and pick you up, dust you off, and cheer you on. He's in your corner! No one wants you to win this battle more than Jesus.

When you get up in the morning, confess this:

Lord, I want a MIND MAKE-OVER today. I dedicate all my thoughts to you. Help me think on pure things and things that please you. Then help me use my mouth to bring peace and encouragement to those around me. Train me in this Lord. Thank you for your help!

GET A BETTER GRIP by reading:
Ephesians 4:17 & 22-25   I Peter 4:7   Romans 8:6   Titus 1:15

What did God speak to me today through this chapter?

What action do I need to take in my life to apply what I have learned?

Chapter 27

Physician Assisted Death
(Dealing with sin in your life)
Colossians 3:5-10

"And that means killing off everything connected with that way of death: sexual promiscuity, impurity, lust, doing whatever you feel like whenever you feel like it, and grabbing whatever attracts your fancy. That's a life shaped by things and feelings instead of by God. It's because of this kind of thing that God is about to explode in anger. It wasn't long ago that you were doing all that stuff and not knowing any better. But you know better now, so make sure it's all gone for good: bad temper, irritability, meanness, profanity, dirty talk. Don't lie to one another. You're done with that old life. It's like a filthy set of ill-fitting clothes you've stripped off and put in the fire. Now you're dressed in a new wardrobe. Every item of your new way of life is custom-made by the Creator, with his label on it. All the old fashions are now obsolete."

I bet you thought this chapter was about euthanasia. It's not, but just to let you know, euthanasia is wrong. It's not 'mercy killing,' but it is killing. Even if a person is determined to die, a doctor has no business participating in the murder of his patient. So! Chew on that for a moment, and let's move on.

God loves <u>life.</u> He gave you yours and He wants you to keep it until He takes you to be with Him.

But God hates <u>sin</u>. Sin destroys life and every good thing about life. So God has given sin the death penalty! And He lists for us here in this scripture many of the **sins that have to die out** in our lives. Let's take a look:

- <u>Sexual immorality</u> – having sexual contact of <u>any</u> kind with a person who is not your husband or wife, looking at porno-graphic pictures or writings, or participating in any form of illicit sex (homosexuality, bestiality, S&M, etc.).
- <u>Impurity</u> – Thinking evil thoughts, having filthy intentions and motives.
- <u>Lust</u> – Sexual passion that begins in the mind . . . to look at someone and think wrong thoughts about them, and/or carry them out.
- <u>Evil Desires</u> – Dwelling on and feeding on wrong thoughts and desires.
- <u>Greed</u> – The desire to have more, to have what is forbidden, to selfishly go after things that were not designed to be yours.
- <u>Anger</u> – A burning inside you that is fueled by unresolved bitterness and resentment.
- <u>Rage</u> – Explosive, angry behavior that erupts and then slowly dissipates.
- <u>Malice</u> – Wanting to do harm or hurt others, either in behavior or with words.
- <u>Slander</u> – Cursing or insulting or saying evil about others.
- <u>Filthy Language</u> – Abusive or dirty language, designed to hurt others or bring roughness and pain to a situation.
- <u>Lying</u> – Being dishonest in any form, whether by speaking it, by giving silent consent, or by leading someone to believe something by maneuvering your words.

Jesus is the ultimate, Holy physician; He brings life and can also cause death. In fact, He <u>wants</u> certain parts of you to die! (The ugly, nasty and hurtful parts!) Those sins listed above are like diseases of the spirit. They cause you to live a 'sick' spiritual life.

No wonder Jesus wants to help you put them to death.

You can't do it by yourself. But Jesus can, through the power of the Holy Spirit that now lives in you. <u>Your</u> part is to 'take off' this old sinful self and 'put on' your new self. How do you do that?

Imagine you have layers of different types of clothing on. They make you hot and uncomfortable, so you <u>take action</u> by removing them, one at a time. <u>You </u>initiate taking them off, by your own will and decision.

God's part is to do the supernatural, giving you a desire to get rid of the old stuff, and strengthening you as you 'put on' His characteristics.

When certain stubborn sins exist in your life, it seems hard to 'take them off.' That is where the power of the 'Ultimate Physician' comes in! He realizes you feel handicapped in that area, like a person without arms trying to take off a sweater. So He immediately sends a helper called the Holy Spirit, a tender, careful assistant who helps you wrestle your way out of stubborn sins. Call on Him when you are struggling to take off those difficult sins. "Jesus! Help! Help me take this off!" He'll always be right there with His power and grace to make sure you will be successful. As long as you are willingly working to throw off your old sin self, you can be certain God is powerfully working to help you.

Don't be discouraged if it takes time to conquer those sins in your life. Jesus will never leave you during the whole process. It may take time for you to get completely free, but as you do your best, Jesus will use the process to make you stronger. That may be hard to understand, but when you look back, you'll see that the process actually was a training camp, a training in holiness!

Jesus loves you deeply. He hates sin, because it will destroy your life. Since He's the Great Physician, He'll work non-stop at driving the disease called sin clear out of your life.

GET A BETTER GRIP by reading:
Romans 5:20-21   I John 1:5-10 & 2:1-17

What did God speak to me today through this chapter?

What action do I need to take in my life to apply what I have learned?

Chapter 28

Just Like Classic Coke
(Prejudice and hatred)
Colossians 3:11

"Words like Jewish and non-Jewish, religious and irreligious, insider and outsider, uncivilized and uncouth, slave and free, mean nothing. From now on everyone is defined by Christ, everyone is included in Christ."

Several years ago the Coca-Cola company introduced the "new Coke." It was a different recipe than the classic Coke drink, and it wasn't very successful. People wanted the <u>real</u> thing, the first pattern, and the original taste. So the company brought back the first recipe and called it "Classic Coke."

When God first created humans, His original plan was for there to be NO distinction between peoples. They were <u>all</u> His creation. Well, sin changed all that.

At some point in history, people decided that a person's color, race, gender, job title, etc. separated them, causing some to seem superior and some inferior.

That was not God's original pattern. Sin warped the plan of God, causing rampant racism and hatred between classes of people.

One of the most phenomenal things about God is that He sets things right that humans have messed up. Through Jesus, He began the work of putting away prejudice and hate. Those who claim Christ as Savior are brought back into line with the original pattern of things.

People of all types are now brothers and sisters through the power of God activated by Jesus Christ. There is no more separation based on color or race or gender or birth place. All people who are in Christ are ONE with each other and with God.

The world must envy this oneness, because no matter what they do, they haven't been able to bring about this peace in their lives. The love of Christ overpowers all former prejudices, and people who were once enemies can stand and worship together in the same church.

If you have operated in any prejudices, lay them down and look at people through God's eyes, for we were originally created to be all for one and one for all.

No longer is it acceptable for you to hold grudges against white people, or black people, or women, or people of another nationality or any others who were created differently from you. God has determined to bring His family into oneness!

Many people who are Christians have yet to fully grasp how important it is to show solidarity with other Christians, especially those of different backgrounds. God wants to reveal to the world the power of reconciliation, and He wants to use the church to unveil that power.

If Christians stubbornly refuse to accept people of another race, nationality or gender, they are operating outside of God's will, and they will be responsible for creating setbacks in the kingdom of God. I would hate to stand before God face to face and have to answer for being hard-hearted towards my fellow Christian.

The body of Christ (the church) has every duty to integrate its services, encourage people to invite those who differ from themselves, and reach out to other communities. The world will be astounded at the progress made by churches when we begin operating in the original plan of God!

God's plan was a classic, perfect for then and perfect for today. If every Christian would rearrange their opinions to line up with

God's plan and God's opinions, the supernatural power of God would visit our churches as a result of living in unity and agreement with God and one another.

GET A BETTER GRIP by reading:
Luke 10:25-37   John 1:43-46

What did God speak to me today through this chapter?

What action do I need to take in my life to apply what I have learned?

Chapter 29

Dress For Success
(Developing spiritual traits)
Colossians 3:12

"So, chosen by God for this new life of love, dress in the wardrobe God picked out for you: compassion, kindness, humility, quiet strength, discipline."

America's big companies tell their employees that in order to be successful, they must dress the part. In other words, don't come in to work looking like a bum! They want their employees to take pride in representing themselves and the company. They want their workers to look sharp!

God has a dress code too, but it isn't an earthly one. He tells us what to take off (we talked about that in chapter #27) and then in this scripture he explains to us what to put on. Fortunately, He provides all the spiritual clothing we need to dress for success. Here are some clothes in His designer series:

- <u>Compassion</u> – being sensitive to the suffering of other people
- <u>Kindness</u> – a softness, not harshness, with an attitude of tenderness towards others
- <u>Humility</u> – the opposite of loving yourself the most
- <u>Gentleness</u> – (quiet strength) not weakness, but an attitude

and behavior that refuses to inflict injury or harm on others.

• <u>Patience</u> – (discipline) Not allowing vengeful thoughts and deep resentments to be the driving force in your life. Quiet waiting; an undisturbed and self-controlled attitude.

These are the "Clothes of Christ." You will notice that each time you wear this spiritual clothing you will look and feel better about yourself.

You will become more and more beautiful, and others will notice that your "wardrobe" has changed and will ask you where they can 'buy' that kind of 'clothing' too!

When you dress in spiritual clothes, you are dressed for ultimate success. These clothes never wear out, never go out of style, and always stay clean. They look elegant and expensive, yet they are trade-ins: trade-ins for your hatred, your mean attitude, your self centered ways, your harshness and your quick temper!

Each morning when you get up and are dressing for the day, 'put on' your designer series God-clothes too.

You'll be amazed how attractive they make you, and you'll be delighted with the success you will experience in relationships.

<u>GET A BETTER GRIP by reading:</u>
2 Peter 1:5-9

What did God speak to me today through this chapter?

What action do I need to take in my life to apply what I have learned?

Chapter 30

So You Want To Be Forgiven. . .
(Forgiving others)
Colossians 3:13

"Be even-tempered, content with second place, quick to forgive an offense. Forgive as quickly and completely as the Master forgave you."

During World War 2 a woman and her family were taken as prisoners and sent to the Nazi death camps. All of her family were cruelly treated and died in the camps before the war was over. She alone survived. Many years afterwards, she was speaking about her experience to a group of Christians.

When she was done with her message, a man approached her. It was none other than the Nazi guard from the German concentration camp. At first, hatred and vengeance filled her heart and she could hardly look at him. Then the Holy Spirit moved upon her, reminding her that if she could not forgive this man <u>his</u> sins, God could not forgive her of her sins. She responded to the Lord's voice, and embraced the man. Instantly, waves of peace and comfort enveloped her.

In forgiving him, she allowed God to forgive her also. The woman was Corrie TenBoom.

Forgiveness is not always easy, nor does it always seem fair. We wonder if the person that hurt us is ever going to pay for their sin. But God has laid down a law in the spiritual world that we have to obey. If we want to <u>be</u> forgiven then we have to forgive. When we live with a desire for revenge or to see people hurt like they hurt us, we haven't yet forgiven.

What are the steps in this process of forgiving?

1. <u>First</u>, believe that God saw everything that happened to you and <u>will</u> bring justice to your situation in <u>His</u> timing.
2. <u>Second</u>, remind yourself of the many, many sins that you have committed against God and other people, and confess to Him that you would be guilty if not for Christ's forgiveness.
3. <u>Third</u>, release that person into God's custody. He can deal with them much better than you can.
4. <u>Fourth</u>, say OUT LOUD "I choose now to forgive _____ for hurting me, and I no longer charge this debt to their account."
5. <u>Fifth</u>, praise and worship the Lord OUT LOUD for setting you free from the control of unforgiveness and bitterness.
6. <u>Sixth</u>, do the first five every day until you are totally free and can truly love that person you've forgiven. Even if it takes days, weeks or months, you will be successful!

Remember, Jesus sees your sins as gone, buried in the depths of the sea. If you choose not to forgive someone, Jesus has no choice but to drag those nasty sins up from the depths and hold you responsible for them.

Forgive others, so you can be forgiven. He loves you so much; He doesn't want the heavy chains of unforgiveness to weigh you down anymore.

Remember, unforgiveness does not mean the person who hurt you is free from responsibility. God will hold them responsible! But you must do as Jesus did, and release them.

"Father, forgive them, for they don't realize what they are doing." Those were Jesus' words while He was still hanging on the cross. Even in the midst of your pain, the Holy Spirit of Jesus can help you whisper those words, and mean them from your heart.

GET A BETTER GRIP by reading:
Matthew 6:9-15   Matthew 18:21-35   Luke 6:37   Luke 23:34

What did God speak to me today through this chapter?

What action do I need to take in my life to apply what I have learned?

Chapter 31

The Love Layer
(Learning to respond with Love)
Colossians 3:14

"And regardless of what else you put on, wear love. It's your basic, all-purpose garment. Never be without it."

You've already read about dressing for success with compassion, kindness, humility, gentleness and patience. Now we want our 'clothes of the spirit' to be complete!

Whether it's spring, fall, winter or a cool summer, you can always wear an expensive, lightweight, tailor-made soft leather coat.

Putting on that classy coat finishes off your look, and you are ready to go anywhere feeling confident and well dressed. That is exactly what we do when we "put on Love." It's the layer that brings it all together, and covers every other piece of 'clothing' we are wearing.

The Love Layer keeps all the other 'clothes' from getting ruined due to bad weather. For example, when it's difficult to be kind to someone who has been tough on you, it's Love that finally motivates you to respond with kindness.

When your patience has been stretched to the limit and you don't feel like you can stand being mistreated one more minute, it's

Love that rescues you and gives you strength to endure.

Love isn't just a romantic feeling or words that flatter. It isn't something you confess when you want to get your way. Love is deeper, richer, filled with meaning and goodness. It's doing the things Jesus did just because it's right. It's considering other people before you consider yourself. It's sacrificing your time and money or talents so that others can benefit.

Love motivates you to grow up and act like a man or woman of God. Love desires to grow in righteousness. Love says "I'm sorry, I was wrong." Love doesn't steal, doesn't fight, and doesn't hold grudges.

Adding the Love Layer to your life isn't an option for a believer. It is THE piece of spiritual clothing we must have to thrive and grow in Christ.

God never promised that Loving would always be easy, or that we would always FEEL like treating others with Love. It's a self-discipline! It's saying "I WILL myself to treat that person with the same love that Jesus shows me."

Once you make the <u>choice</u> to Love, you free up God's spirit on the inside of you to act supernaturally on your behalf to <u>help</u> you Love.

You see, Love is a protection against the elements of the world, just like your prized leather coat is a shield against driving rain and cold. When you make the choice to Love, immediately you have the protection of the Holy Spirit surrounding you!

For instance, if your friend knowingly and willingly hurts you, you might be tempted to get revenge. If you choose to respond in gentleness instead, God's protection and mighty hand begin to act powerfully on your behalf.

In other words, Love fights our battles for us! God IS Love, and when we walk in His spirit of Love we are allowing the powers of heaven to line up behind us. What an incredible thought!

So 'put on' the Love Layer each day. Get to the point where you feel naked without it! Ask God to teach you how to Love, and then obey Him even when it's challenging. You'll find yourself filled with joy when you can respond in Love instead of in anger or bitterness.

If you get discouraged when you fail to be loving, pick yourself up, admit to doing wrong, and start again.

That pleases God, because He loves you deeply, and wants to train you in this process of learning to Love others with True Love.

GET A BETTER GRIP by reading:
I Corinthians 13   I John 3:11-18   I John 4:7-21

What did God speak to me today through this chapter?

What action do I need to take in my life to apply what I have learned?

Chapter 32

You <u>Can</u> Live A Peaceful Life
Colossians 3:15

"Let the peace of Christ keep you in tune with each other, in step with each other. None of this going off and doing your own thing. And cultivate thankfulness."

The only time some people experience peace is when they are lying under a headstone titled "REST IN PEACE." (And that's only if they make it to heaven!)

God never intended your life to be a whirlwind of anxiety, trouble and stress. John 10:10 tells us that God wants to give us a life that is "superabundant in quantity and superior in quality." That is why He sent Jesus, so that the thief (satan) of your quantity and quality of life might be defeated.

When you and I live in distress, fighting and trouble we are not taking advantage of the great inheritance that Jesus left for us, and that is a life of peace. We will always encounter some difficult circumstances in life, and there will always be challenging people to deal with. Even with these things, God has assured us that it is possible to live peacefully.

How can you begin experiencing this peace every day of your life?

First of all, start by practicing thankfulness. Express to God and others all the things for which you are grateful. Instead of using critical words and looking for the negative, begin looking for the positive in people and circumstances. Say these positive and thankful words out loud to yourself and to others.

Second, (Psalm 34:14) make a choice to reject doing evil, and instead choose to pursue (run after) peace. That means to look ahead and see which path leads to a peaceful end, and take that course.

Third, (Psalm 120:6) stop hanging out with those who hate peace.

Fourth, (Isaiah 26:3) keep your thoughts in line with peace. As soon as you start thinking thoughts that cause you anxiety or stress, determine to set your mind on thinking thoughts that bring you peace.

Fifth, (Isaiah 48:8) pay attention and obey the commands of the Lord. It's not enough to just hear what the commands of God are. You must follow through and obey what you know is right. No excuses.

Sixth, (Philippians 4:4) Spend time praising your God, and praying about what concerns you. Trust Him with that prayer and leave your problem with Him. When you are tempted to take it up again, remember it's too heavy for you to lift, and your back wasn't made to carry that heavy load! Let Jesus have it again.

Last of all, forgive and move on! The resentments you have been harboring in your heart towards someone is stealing your peace. Let it go!

If you want to enjoy the life of peace that God has PROMISED to His people, practice these things, and continue practicing them.

And the God Who Is Peace will always be present with you to help you retain the peace He died to give you.

GET A BETTER GRIP by reading:
John 14:27   Psalm 29:11   Isaiah 48:18   John 16:33

What did God speak to me today through this chapter?

What action do I need to take in my life to apply what I have learned?

Chapter 33

Get Rich Quick!
(How and why you need to read God's Word)
Colossians 3:16

"Let the Word of Christ—the Message—have the run of the house. Give it plenty of room in your lives. Instruct and direct one another using good common sense. And sing, sing your hearts out to God!"

Most people have, at one time or another in their lifetime, dreamed of being wealthy. What would it be like to have abundance at your fingertips? How would it feel to have plenty of everything?

Living lavishly sounds so inviting. But some of the same people who have all they want in the material world are desperately poor in the spirit world. They don't know Christ or His Word or the freedom that comes from being content with what they have.

So basically, they aren't really RICH. They may have fat bank accounts, but true riches come from hearing God's voice through His Word, receiving His promises, and being changed into a man or woman of integrity. (Now that's a person who can rejoice when they look at themselves in the mirror each morning!)

How can you live life as a truly rich person? Fill yourself up with the Word of God, the Bible. It will permeate every area of your life and bring freshness, wholeness and newness to you. It will add, and keep adding to you the treasures of wisdom, knowledge and guidance.

Read it, listen to it on tape, and pay attention to the Word being preached. Surround yourself with songs that sing the Word. It's like gobbling 10 trillion Vitamin C's . . . it brings health to every part of your life.

Some folks might tease you or hurt you with comments like "You're being brainwashed!" You can smile right back at 'em and say "Yep, my brain needed a good cleaning!"

You see, the supernatural power of the Word will change you little by little each time you hear it and take it in. You may not feel anything different, but you will notice as days pass that the Word which is dwelling (living alive) in you IS working and transforming every part of your life.

So, you want to get RICH quick? Spend as much time in the Word of God that you can, and watch it change you, your circumstances, your attitudes, your reactions, your relationships.

When Jesus left the earth He 'willed' you the Word as your priceless inheritance. If you let it sit on your coffee table, it's just the same as if your grandfather willed you a billion dollars and you let it sit in a bank account untouched. Use it! That's what it's there for!

God has given you all the riches in the heavenly realms, and promised to take care of all your material needs 'according to His riches' also. We absolutely have it all, and it's always at our fingertips.

Open the Word, and get rich quick. Oh, incidentally, even those lucky lottery winners eventually spend all their money, and they are poor once more. The Word is the only treasure that is endless; the more you discover, the richer you become.

Here's how to start reading God's Word:

1. Begin in the New Testament. The Bible has Old and New Testaments, and the New Testament introduces Jesus Christ.

2. Ask God to help you understand what you are about to read.

3. Start in the book of Colossians. Read one chapter a day (It will take 5-7 minutes). Write down your thoughts in a journal.

4. During the day, meditate and think about what God's Word taught you.

5. When you are done with the book of Colossians, begin reading the Book of Matthew. (The first Book in the New Testament). Read one chapter per day, continuing to use your journal to record your thoughts, and read through to the end of the Book of Revelation (The end of the Bible).

6. You may want to purchase a devotional, which is a daily spiritual help guide. Any Christian bookstore in your area or online will carry a full line of specialized devotionals tailored to your interests.

GET A BETTER GRIP by reading:
Hebrews 4:12   Romans 15:4 I   John 5:13   Acts 17:11

What did God speak to me today through this chapter?

What action do I need to take in my life to apply what I have learned?

Chapter 34

Who is the Holy Spirit and How Will He Help Me?
(Baptism with the Holy Spirit)
Colossians 3:17

"Let every detail in your lives—words, actions, whatever—be done in the name of the Master, Jesus, thanking God the Father every step of the way."

It happened suddenly! Jesus had already been resurrected and He told his followers to wait in Jerusalem for the gift He would give them. So these men and woman, friends and believers in Jesus, gathered together in one place.

Suddenly a violent wind began to blow! Flames of fire came down from heaven and blazed above their heads! Jesus carried out what He had promised: He poured out His powerful spirit, baptizing these believers with the Holy Spirit and fire. They were each (men and women) filled with the Holy Spirit and began to speak in other languages (tongues) as the spirit enabled them.

People in Jerusalem who were watching and listening began to laugh and joke. "These folks are drunk!" Then Peter, one of the 12 close followers of Christ, spoke up to explain. "We aren't drunk like you think," he exclaimed. "God said this would happen! He said that in the final days He would pour out His spirit on men and women, the old and the young! These believers are not drunk with alcohol; they are filled with the spirit of the living God!"

Apparently these believers were filled with joy, and were speaking with words no one had taught them, so the onlookers thought they were drunk. They could not have been more wrong! These believers were under the influence of a powerful God.

Jesus poured out His Holy Spirit upon His friends because He wanted them to have supernatural courage, power and love so they wouldn't be afraid to be a bold witness for him.

He wanted them to be completely consumed, not with wine or alcohol, but with the incredible power of the Holy Spirit! And He wants the same for you and me and every other believer.

Jesus also wanted to give them (and us) the ability to fulfill Colossians 3:17 – "Whatever you do, whether in word or deed, do it all in the name of the Lord Jesus." (NIV Translation)

Those early disciples, just like us, lived in a morally corrupt environment. Every kind of sin was happening all around them and temptation was on every hand. God wanted to give His people power to overcome sin and power to be examples to those around them.

When believers feed the poor or perform other good deeds, we are doing it to expose the name and the glory of Jesus to other people. When we refuse to take part in sin, we are honoring the name of Jesus in front of others. The power and courage to do these things is given to us by the Holy Spirit. He filled the first century believers, and He wants to fill you also!

To receive Jesus' gift of the Holy Spirit (commonly called the "Baptism with the Holy Spirit," Acts 1:5) all you have to do is ASK! Say "Jesus, come baptize me with your Holy Spirit; accomplish your will in my life by furnishing your power and boldness to me. I accept the gift of your Spirit by faith in your name."

Often, it is when you are worshipping Jesus and focused on him alone that you will receive this baptism.

Remember, when you are seeking and asking God for this 'baptism,' you are requesting that His son Jesus grant you the gift of the Holy Spirit. Don't just seek the gift for the novelty of seeing if it will happen, and don't seek this gift so you can speak in tongues.

The Holy Spirit is a <u>personal being</u>, not some 'rush' or some supernatural adventure. He is the very essence of Jesus, wanting to empower you and enable you to follow God in every area of your life.

And don't be afraid of the 'tongues' thing. God would not give you something weird or fearful. In fact, there are some important purposes for the spiritual language God wants to give you as evidence of the Holy Spirit's presence in your life.

I Corinthians Chapter 14 verses, 2, 4, 5, 18 teach us that:

1. Tongues are used as a witness to others
2. Speaking in tongues builds up your faith
3. Anyone can speak in tongues who has been baptized with the Holy Spirit
4. You can thank God that you speak in tongues no matter what others think or say!

All believers in Jesus can be baptized with the Holy Spirit, regardless of their past life or their previous religious traditions. God loves everyone equally, and will give the gift of His Holy Spirit to all who believe.

Luke 11:11 records Jesus teaching his disciples to pray and ask their Father in heaven to give them the Holy Spirit: "Which of you fathers, if your son asks for a fish, will give him a snake instead? Or if he asks for an egg, will give him a scorpion? If you then, though you are evil, know how to give good gifts to your children, how much more will your Father in heaven give the <u>Holy Spirit</u> to those who ask him."

GET A BETTER GRIP by reading:
Acts 2:1-41   Acts 5:32   Acts 8:14-17   Acts 10:44-47

What did God speak to me today through this chapter?

What action do I need to take in my life to apply what I have learned?

Chapter 35

Wives Who Win

Colossians 3:18

"Wives, understand and support your husbands by submitting to them in ways that honor the Master."

A wife came home one evening with a huge smile on her face. "Honey, I won the lottery!" she said. "Pack your bags!"

"That's incredible!" he shouted. "I'll go pack. Are we going to the mountains or the seashore?"

"Just pack your bags," she replied, "you're outta here!"

So many wives and husbands live in emotional poverty. They want to be happily married, but they don't know how to fix all the problems in their relationship. They opt for divorce, thinking that freedom or another relationship will provide what they've been missing. Most of the time they're dead wrong.

Fortunately, God has provided the blueprints for successful marriage relationships. If we study those blueprints and follow them closely, we are on the way to building a stable, more mature marriage.

God is on your side! He wants to provide a way to WIN the battle that rages for your marriage. But you have to decide beforehand that you are willing to play by <u>His</u> rules and not your own.

(Take a look and evaluate: has YOUR way proved successful?)

First of all, let's get this straight: wives are not to be abused, whether physically, sexually or with words. They are not supposed to "just sit back and take it." But, while God did not create wives to be mousepads, He also did not create them to be the head, the ruler, and the leading authority figure in a marriage. God <u>does</u> expect each wife to know and understand her important role in her marriage relationship.

As a wife, you are not meant to be inferior or to have a less important role. God has given females certain wonderful gifts that can be used to fulfill both herself and her husband if those gifts are not twisted and warped by wrong thinking.

Scripture indicates that wives are to "submit" to their husbands so that God will be honored. Women absolutely hate this word, mostly because they don't understand it and also because men have used it to belittle women. Even Christian women don't want to hear the word "submit" because they think it means they have to be some kind of slave. WRONG.

Once again, the devil, the consummate enemy of the family, has almost successfully blinded the minds of women so they will rebel against the very word which can set them free.

God wants wives to <u>win</u>, to be free, to be protected, and to experience fulfillment and wholeness as a wife. Jesus Christ elevated the status of women from the moment He was conceived (Mary was honored above every living human being), until His resurrection, when He granted a woman (Mary of Magdala) the privilege of seeing and speaking with Him before anyone else.

Jesus consistently offered grace, compassion and complete respect to every woman He encountered. In a culture that devalued women, He allowed women to be among His closest supporters. Jesus has done more for the advancement of women than anyone else in the history of the world! He successfully challenged the tradition that women were second class citizens in society, and proved Himself their greatest champion!

So, back to the word 'submit.' God has established principles to ensure that a woman will succeed in her marriage no matter what the circumstances, or in which century she lives! The truths in the

Bible about wives and husbands are timeless.

There are some religious wackos who distort the teachings of God about the duty of a wife, but just ignore them. You can trust God's way of doing things. God's plan is for ALL human beings to be valued, respected and elevated to their highest level.

'Submit' means to be tender to your husband, to offer your advice and opinion but to yield to his final decision as the one who has to give account to the Lord. It means to adapt yourself to not demanding your own way. It means respecting his authority as the head of the home, and trusting God to work with your husband no matter what his spiritual condition.

In Ephesians 5:33, God gives women the key to receiving the love they need from their husbands. When a woman treats her husband respectfully, it suddenly sparks in her husband a desire to love his wife, granting her the affection and attention she craves.

A submissive, respectful, spirit is a kind and gentle spirit, not a weak or pitiful one. It is courteous and considerate, willingly working with a husband to determine the best course of action.

Submission is a spiritual law, and when you as a wife operate in submission, you set free the power of the Word of God to work in your marriage.

When you rebel and refuse to be respectful and submissive, you are binding the very spiritual help that you need to make your marriage a success! Being mouthy, obnoxious and stubborn will never bring you happiness in your marriage. It will make both of you miserable, and will accomplish nothing.

If you examine respect and submission truthfully, you will see that they are principles designed to set you free from a life of anxiety. God will deal with your husband, but not if you always throw yourself in the way.

Women are afraid to offer respect and submit because they are afraid of being run over. In reality, in the context of a marriage where there is not abuse, respect and submission actually elevate the position of a wife to that of a wise support, a counselor, a trusted advisor, and a friend. She is viewed by her husband as an active participant in decision making without being domineering.

She is free from carrying the weight of the family headship.

God would never have designed a family plan that would crush women. Women are not required to submit to do evil things, things that violate God's Word, or activities that would cause them to compromise their Christian life. If a husband asks his wife to sin on his behalf, she has every right to vigorously refuse! That's not submission, that's domination! He would be out of God's will and walking in disobedience to God's commands to force his wife to sin in any way.

Jesus' plan for the family is trustworthy! A wife that adapts, yields, respects and submits herself to her husband will live in peace and can count on God to be her protector. On the other hand, a wife who fights her own battles, insists on having her own way, and refuses to respect and listen to her husband will end up bitter and lonely.

Often, if a woman is married to a grumpy, controlling jerk of a guy, she feels she has a right to be exempted from God's 'respect and submission' plan. Just the opposite! God says "There are husbands who, indifferent as they are to any words about God, will be captivated by your life of holy beauty, your inner-disposition." (I Peter 3:1, The Message)

The 'holy beauty' is the life of Christ shining from the inside out. That will make a woman so very attractive to her husband, that in time he will get hungry for the things of God.

You can trust and rely on God's perfect plan for wives. He wants you to win the battle for your marriage so you can live a happy, fulfilled life!

GET A BETTER GRIP by reading:
I Corinthians Chapter 7   Ephesians 5:22   Mark 10:9
I Peter 3:1-7

What did God speak to me today through this chapter?

What action do I need to take in my life to apply what I have learned?

Chapter 36

Home-Hearted Husbands
Colossians 3:19

"Husbands, go all out in love for your wives. Don't take advantage of them."

There is no joy in being a half-hearted husband! The husband who only loves his wife when it's convenient or when he wants sex is missing out on a <u>complete</u> life. God designed the woman to complete a man's life, not subtract from it. If you have been shown a poor example of what a husband should be, someone has cheated you out of a whole lot of happiness.

Think of your wife as being an "empty pitcher." Fill that pitcher with vinegar, and when you reach for it to take a drink you'll get a mouthful of bitterness. But if you fill that pitcher with honey, you'll sip sweetness and enjoy renewed energy. In other words, pouring love into your wife actually strengthens and invigorates you as a husband.

Paul's words here are not a suggestion. They are a direct instruction to those men who were trying to understand the "new way of life" they had in Christ Jesus. His words presented a whole new way of thinking for the husbands in the new testament church.

When Paul writes "love your wives as Christ loved the church" (Ephesians 5:25) he means that a husband is to love his wife in spite of her failings, and is not to be harsh and demanding with her. This kind of love is self-sacrificing (as Christ's love is) and is committed to protecting and being gentle with a wife. Jesus has given His power to husbands to treat their wives respectfully and graciously, because when others observe a Christian husband's behavior, they see an example of the way Christ loves his people, and they are drawn to Christianity.

Jesus always treats His people with dignity and honor, even though we have done nothing to deserve that treatment. Husbands, as the head of the home, have a grave responsibility before God to imitate Jesus' behavior with their wives. They cannot excuse bad behavior towards their wives by insisting that she doesn't deserve to be treated with love. None of us deserved to be given the love of God while we were still sinning, but God gave us that love freely through His Son Jesus.

Real love is seeking the best for your wife, helping her grow and develop in all areas, and committing yourself only to her for a lifetime. Real love doesn't stay angry and bitter, but forgives and works to reconcile. Loving your wife is like loving your own body. Love her well, and she will meet the needs that you have. Ignore her, neglect her, or treat her harshly, and soon you will find <u>yourself</u> in serious shape.

Remember, your children are watching everything that goes on in your home. They are learning what it means to be a husband and a wife, and they will live out your example in their own lives.

If you feel you have been a poor example, it's not too late! Start right now! Repent before God for not obeying Biblical guidelines for husbands. Go to your wife and apologize, asking her forgiveness, and assure her your desire is to pursue a godly marriage relationship. (It's tempting to think of all the ways in which your wife has failed to obey biblical directives for wives, but you as the husband are the leader, and God wants you to initiate the restoration process! Remember, leaders lead by going first!)

Most wives would be very open to a husband who approached her in that way. However, in cases where a marriage relationship is seriously troubled, a husband must be patient and wait for his wife to SEE the changes in his life for her to believe he is serious about his decision to follow godly principles.

God can deliver any man from addictions that have harmed his marriage. He can restore broken marriage relationships and renew trust between a husband and wife. The power of the Holy Spirit is available to every husband, so call on His name and cry out to Him for help. If you want to be free from any type of addictions, ask God for that freedom. The Bible promises "If the Son sets you free you will be free indeed!" (John 8:36)

Jesus Christ was the model of humility. He treated everyone with a gentle humility that made him approachable. Have you walked in humility in your marriage relationship, or have you been prideful and arrogant? Have you insisted on being right, being in control, or shoving your weight around? Have you displayed an angry and contentious temperament? If you said yes to any of the above, God wants to re-train you to live a life of humility. That does not mean being a wimp, a coward, or a weak leader. Jesus Christ was none of those things.

Humility means considering yourself blessed that God has forgiven your sins, and treating other people in the excessively gracious way in which God is treating you.

A husband is never to mistreat his wife by verbally, physically or sexually abusing her. His duty is to care for her needs, to provide physical and emotional comfort and security, and to protect her from being hurt. He is never to lead her into sin or to encourage her to engage in any behavior that she finds uncomfortable or degrading. He must use his words to build her up, to encourage her, to bring her joy.

A man who truly wants to be the leader in his home must make the effort and take the initiative to restore peace between his wife and himself. Men who say "I'll wait until she makes the first move" aren't leaders at all, they are followers. God expects His men to be leaders in their homes, taking the first step towards rekindling love.

Becoming a godly husband will take time and effort, but with God's help you will become the kind of husband your wife will adore. A home-hearted husband will win the respect of his family and his community. But best of all, God will be pleased and bless the husband who chooses to live by His principles.

GET A BETTER GRIP by reading:
Ephesians 5:25-33   I Peter 3:7   I Corinthians Chapter 7
Jeremiah 3:14,   The Book of Hosea

What did God speak to me today through this chapter?

What action do I need to take in my life to apply what I have learned?

Chapter 37

Raising Successful Children
Colossians 3:20

"Children, do what your parents tell you. This delights the
Master to no end."

Every good parent wants their child to succeed. Most parents
hope for good grades, the right kind of friends, and a college
education for their children. But these days, so many "good" kids
seem to go bad. They experiment with drugs, premarital sex, and
other dangerous activities. What can you do as parents to see to it
that your children are raised to succeed in life and not to fail? Here
are some Bible-based suggestions to help you get started.

Understand this is only a beginning point, but perhaps these
ideas will catapult you into fresh new thinking about the way you
are raising your children.

1. Show your child unconditional love, especially when she
   messes up. Reassure her that you accept her when she fails.

2. Give your child proper physical affection, even through their
   teen years. Hugs and kisses on the cheek and pats on the back
   and hand all speak of your love.

3. Teach your children to honor the Word of God by reading and memorizing it with them.

4. Take your children to church with you on regular basis. Don't send them alone, go with them! Send them the message that God is your first priority.

5. Set standards and rules in your household, and apply appropriate punishment when they are broken. Be consistent! Don't let your children rule your house!

6. Don't play favorites in any way between your children.

7. Don't criticize your children in front of others.

8. Be liberal with words of sincere praise and encouragement. Find the good in everything they do and focus on it. Use your words to create things in your child that you would like to see instead of being critical and negative.

9. Provide, according to your financial means, for all their physical <u>needs</u> (Not all their wants!).

10. Give your children focused attention daily. Look into their eyes, listen while they are speaking, and answer back. Turn off the TV, computer, and all other distractions and play games, sports, or other activities your children enjoy.

11. Discipline your children only after you are in control of your anger. You don't have to be hostile to let them know you mean business. Be firm, be fair, and don't ignore their backtalk, misbehavior and disobedience. Discipline according to their age. (Great books are available on parenting from Focus on the Family, Dr. James Dobson.)

12. Teach your child to obey the FIRST time they are asked to do something. In our home, we call this 'first-time obedience.'

13. Follow the Golden Rule: treat your child like you want to be treated.

14. Teach your children to be orderly. Get them a personal alarm clock, teach them to pick up their room before they leave home, and give them daily and weekly chores.

15. Don't allow your children to be sassy and talk back to you in a disrespectful manner. Firmly declare that they will be required to treat you with respect in their words, attitudes, and behavior. If they don't, follow up immediately with correction, both verbally and with appropriate punishment.

16. Pray for your children daily. Declare the blood of Jesus is their protection, and believe God for their salvation and for needed changes in their lives.

17. Be involved in your children's lives. Know what they are doing, who they are with. Don't assume they can train themselves to make right choices. Be there to give them guidance and leadership. Don't be an absentee parent! If you must give up a job or a hobby to be with your children more, then by all means do it!

18. Be involved in the school your children attend. Know what is happening and the lessons which are being taught. Watch carefully for "culturally correct" moral teachings that conflict with biblical principles. Make certain your children know right from wrong as taught in God's Word.

God loves parents . . . HE is one! And He wants to teach you to parent your children so they will grow up to succeed and obey and serve Him. He will help you! Find a local church that offers parenting classes and attend regularly. Ask the Holy Spirit for daily help and wisdom and He will gladly answer.

GET A BETTER GRIP BY READING:
Proverbs 22:6 2 Corinthians 12:14 Ephesians 6:4 Proverbs 13:24 Proverbs 19:18 Proverbs 22:15 Deuteronomy 31:13

Did God speak to me today through this chapter?

What action do I need to take in my life to apply what I have learned?

Chapter 38

Foundations For Fatherhood
(How to be a great dad to your children)
Colossians 3:21

"Parents, don't come down too hard on your children or you'll crush their spirits."

Do you remember when you were a kid? I bet you can clearly remember a time when at least one parent exasperated and irritated you by treating you with contempt, speaking hurtful words to you or otherwise pushing you to the edge by their behavior. God's Word reveals that when parents do that to their children, they are hurting them in a way that could seriously damage their relationship and effect that child's future.

One sure way to discourage your children is to nag them and continually irritate them with your words and behavior. This scripture actually says to avoid stirring up and provoking your children, which leads them to lose heart and become discouraged. When they become discouraged, they are more likely to become involved in harmful activities and make friends with people (even nasty people) they think will accept them.

If you were mistreated by a parent, then chances are you are mistreating your children in many of the same ways. Perhaps your parents were not saved and therefore did not know the Biblical way to raise children. But now <u>you</u> are a new Christian, and you must to treat your children in a way that would please Jesus Christ.

Practice your Christian parenting by determining to end any behavior that would demoralize your children. Check your words, attitudes and actions to see which ones seem to crush the life out of your children. Then stop yourself before you say or do something that would be harmful, and leave the room until you regain control of yourself. When you finally confront your child, watch your tone of voice, and ask yourself "How can I address this ISSUE and not demean my child?"

When you are old and gray, I bet you'll want your children to love you and want to have you around. If so, think about that <u>now</u>, and treat your child with respect. When you do, they will respect you and desire a relationship with you for a lifetime.

There will be times you will fail, and you will need to apologize to your child for treating him/her poorly. That will bring you closer together, and will help your child understand how important it is to say "I'm sorry."

This scripture addresses 'fathers' very specifically. Fathers are supposed to be a protector, leader, and gentle helper to their children. Fathers can build up or destroy their child's self-worth, so it is very important for fathers to 'bless' their children and not 'curse' them. God wants fathers to reflect His love and His behavior, and when they do, children are naturally drawn to a relationship with their heavenly father.

If you have been part of a family where abusive behavior, immoral lifestyles, and addictions were part of your life, you CAN break the patterns you have seen by obeying God's Word, practicing it daily. You don't have to be the kind of father your own father was. God has the power to destroy the works of the devil, and to help you start a fresh family life.

Even if your dad did not know the best way (God's way) to father you, you now have the opportunity to treat your children with the respect and deep affection you might have missed in your childhood.

Father's are the 'covering' for the home. They 'uncover' their children when they choose to engage in sinful behavior, and they open up their children to involvement in the same sins. If fathers live a life of purity, they are 'covering' their children, acting as a wall of protection against sin.

It is critically important for fathers to take responsibility for their children. Some fathers let their wives do all the parenting, setting their children up for failure. Fathers must be 'daily' participants in the parenting process.

God has selected fathers to lead their children and their wives spiritually. If the wife/mother is the one leading the family to church, leading them in prayer, and attempting to train the children morally without dad's involvement, the children are losing out.

So dad, get in there and get involved in your children's lives: in school, at home, in church, in sports. Support their interests. Be a daily dad!

Concentrate on and memorize the scriptures that highlight fathering. Allow them to re-train your mind and re-form your attitude about parenting. You can do it! God will help you.

GET A BETTER GRIP by reading:
Luke 1:17   Ephesians 6:4   Hebrews 12:9   Psalm 103:13

What did God speak to me today through this chapter?

What action do I need to take in my life to apply what I have learned?

Chapter 39

Serving God on the Job
Colossians 3:22-25

"Servants, do what you're told by your earthly masters. And don't just do the minimum that will get you by. Do your best. Work from the heart for your real Master, for God, confident that you'll get paid in full when you come into your inheritance. Keep in mind always that the ultimate Master you're serving is Christ. The sullen servant who does shoddy work will be held responsible. Being Christian doesn't cover up bad work."

We've all had jobs that made us feel like we were slaves rather than well-paid, respected employees. Maybe you have felt under-appreciated and taken advantage of, which opens the door for the temptation to deal dishonestly with your employer. God will allow you to be in job situations that are not easy in order to test what is in your heart. Are you sincerely attempting to serve God by serving your employer well, or are you justifying bad behavior by blaming your employer for the way he/she treats you?

You see, God even rewards us for doing good work on the job, not just for activities done in church or in Christian service. He wants you to take your employment seriously, working hard and faithfully, so He can reward you. If God sees that you are doing your best, being honest, taking initiative, serving your employer faithfully, He will reward you in many ways. Perhaps He will see to it that you get a promotion, or receive an unexpected raise. Or maybe He will open up another employment opportunity, and reward you with a fresh start.

He wants you to be obedient to your employer's instructions, as long as they are legal and don't violate your Christian conscience. Instead of giving your boss a hassle and being disrespectful, God wants you to have a positive attitude and a willing spirit. Even when your boss isn't around, God wants you to work diligently, because it honors Him.

Every day you go in to work, remind yourself that you really have a heavenly boss who is watching and recording all that you do, so that in the future He can promote you and reward you. It is really Jesus you are serving when you do a good job, not your employer.

Some people get hung up because they dislike their employer and they feel justified in cutting corners and being lazy. They don't realize that God promises to pay back wrong for wrong! If you cheat your employer, you will be cheated. If you are slothful or negligent, others will take advantage of you in the same way.

Also, don't use your Christianity as an excuse for disobedience and wrongdoing. Don't use it as a cover-up or a shield. Come clean and be honest and trustworthy, and others will learn that you can be trusted.

Even when you have a nasty boss, God expects you to be a man or woman of character and integrity. In that way you reveal Jesus to others who may have no other way of knowing Him. He has your future in His hands, and He will work all things for your good if you will obey Him first. He won't forget your work or labors! He has very special rewards for those who are faithful.

GET A BETTER GRIP by reading:

Titus 2:9-10   Ephesians 5:8

What did God speak to me today through this chapter?

What action do I need to take in my life to apply what I have learned?

Chapter 40

How to be Successful as an Employer
Colossians 4:1

"And masters, treat your servants considerately. Be fair with them. Don't forget for a minute that you, too, serve a Master— God in heaven."

The all-time meaningful buzz words in the business community are "it's a dog eat dog world." Corporations and small businesses alike are consumed with getting ahead, besting the competition, and pulling down big profits. All too often the employee gets lost in the cycle.

Businesses are always looking for ways to improve management and get the most out of their people. They are forever buying books and attending expensive seminars to discover the latest slick technique that might propel them into the big leagues.

Well, hello . . . are you ready for this? The BIBLE has the ANSWER! And it won't cost you a nickel to retrieve it nor a penny to put it into action. But it <u>is costly</u>! It will cost <u>you</u>, as an employer, your bad habits, your cheapskate ways and your lack of integrity. If you have the guts to read on, I'll give you the good news!

When you begin operating by the **<u>GOLDEN RULE</u>** (Do to others what you want them to do to you) you will start to see a

FANTASTIC TURN AROUND in your operations. Your plant moral will skyrocket, your production rate will accelerate, and you will keep those talented employees. Things you have been dreaming about will begin to happen! Even when the economy is in tough times, your business will stay afloat and God will bless it and protect it.

So, what exactly does it mean to operate your business by the Golden Rule? Let me strongly recommend this new business plan to you:

1. Provide your employees with what is right and fair. Stop quibbling over small things, stop scrimping on safety equipment and legitimate needs. Start doing what you know is right by your workers.

2. Pay them what they are worth, or make up the difference by offering special incentives or benefits.

3. When they have a grievance against you, consider what part of their complaint is true. Act upon it with honesty and integrity.

4. Instead of manipulating and threatening workers, co-operate and converse. Treat them as human beings who have creativity and worthwhile ideas.

5. Every time you open your mouth, ask yourself, "Would I like someone to say these things to me?" Check your attitude, your tone of voice, and your mannerisms. Do they build up or tear down?

6. Put people above money, and you will make money with people.

7. Encourage your employees with kind words and sincere compliments. If you are a 'hard-driving' type of boss, cushion your in-your-face style with positive observations. Everybody responds to uplifting words!

8. Get rid of dishonesty, cheating, and false book-keeping and other types of moral corruptions. Honor God in your business practices, and He will honor you with prosperity.

9. Pay the taxes you owe the government. Pay the social security you owe for your workers. Report the taxable income you make. If you are responsible to do it, withhold monies for child support from delinquent parent-employees.

10. Don't cut corners while producing your marketable item. Back up the claims you make in your advertisements with product integrity. Make sure your employees know they are to create the highest quality product and make it safe and profitable for them to do so.

You are the master of your business. You can use your authority harshly or with compassion and justice. Either way, you need to remember that you <u>also</u> have a master, and He is always watching and taking note of your behavior.

If you allow Him to be your master, your Lord, and your ultimate guide, then you will be a phenomenal employer. You will please Him and please your workers at the same time. It's a win-win deal.

Trash any advice that places money before people. Employers who worship their bottom line will never be truly successful. That kind of business style always alienates people and eventually leads to failure and emptiness.

Producing goods and services to help people and honor God, while at the same time making a good living for your family, should be the aim of the God-centered business.

The man or woman who makes Jesus Christ the chief executive officer of their business will be an ultimate achiever.

GET A BETTER GRIP by reading:
Job 31:13-28   Ephesians 6:9

What did God speak to me today through this chapter?

What action do I need to take in my life to apply what I have learned?

Chapter 41

Call Him Up: Learning How to Pray

Colossians 4:2-4

"Pray diligently. Stay alert, with your eyes wide open in gratitude. Don't forget to pray for us, that God will open doors for
telling the mystery of Christ, even while I'm locked up in this
jail. Pray that every time I open my mouth I'll be able to make
Christ plain as day to them."

We used to sing these words in a chorus: "If you confess the
Lord, call Him up!" As a committed believer, you need to
grab the concept of prayer: what to pray, how to pray, where to pray,
who to pray for, and when to pray!

Prayer is calling on God, your all-powerful friend, so you can
learn to trust Him for everything. He designed prayer as a way to tie
you close to Him and teach you to communicate in the supernatural
world.

When you pray, just speak to Jesus as if you could touch and see
Him, and simply talk to Him about anything in your life. You don't
need to wear anything special, or say any certain words or sit in any
particular position to get God's attention. He hears you the moment
you cry out to Him.

You can pray about ANYTHING that concerns you. Ask Him to
provide for your needs, to lead you in decision making, to show you

how to change things in your life. And be open to the things He wants to say back to <u>you</u>. He wants to talk to you and get through to you just as much as you want to get through to Him.

God wants you to stay in contact with Him all day, every day. You can pray in an elevator, a car, while you shave or in a business meeting. You can breathe a short prayer or spend time really connecting with Him on a subject. You can let out frustrations to Him (He knows them all anyway) and tell Him how you really feel. He isn't startled by your prayers or your feelings and He won't put you down when you express them.

Prayer is night and day communication, it's daily conversation <u>and</u> emergency counseling! That's because it's a RELATIONSHIP thing. Anytime, anywhere, for any reason, God wants to hear from you. He is a Father that WANTS to listen to you. And He's a Father that wants to let you know He is answering, no matter what circumstances may look like around you.

God wants you to learn how to pray without giving up. He wants you to hold on like a pit bull to your requests. He will teach you how to have faith while you wait for your answer. His desire is that you pray and not give up! By doing so, you are exercising spiritual muscles that may be weak at first but with constant use become strong and ripped, ready for anything.

Prayer to a Christian is trading in our problems for His peace, and our frustrations for His directions. We cannot survive as a Christian without praying. He planned it that way because He wants to share in our lives everyday.

Here is an easy 4 step prayer plan which will help you get started praying regularly: Simply remember the acronym 'ACTS'. . .

1. **A-Adoration**: worship the Lord and share your affection and love for Him.

2. **C-Confession**: confess your sins, both the ones you know and the ones you've forgotten.

3. **T-Thanksgiving**: give God thanks for all He's done and

what He's about to do in your life.

4. **<u>S-Supplication</u>**: ask Him to supply the needs in your life and the lives of your friends and family and others. Pray for your pastor, your church, and your nation.

You can remember to pray ACTS anytime and anywhere, it's a simple way to begin your intimate journey getting to know God.

Don't ignore Him; each day He patiently waits for you to "call Him up" to talk!

GET A BETTER GRIP by reading:
Matthew 6:5-15   Luke 18:1-8   Philippians 4:6-7

What did God speak to me today through this chapter?

What action do I need to take in my life to apply what I have learned?

Chapter 42

Now That I'm a Christian,
How Should I Act Around Others?
Colossians 4:5

"Use your heads as you live and work among outsiders. Don't
miss a trick. Make the most of every opportunity."

When your life takes a dramatic turn other people will notice.
They may even give you a hard time or ask you a lot of
questions about the changes they see in you.

Take advantage of every opportunity you have to share what
Jesus has done for you! Don't be afraid to speak up and give Him
the credit for changing your life. Other people who need Him will
hear your words and get hungry for what you have.

At the same time, it is important for you to be wise in the way
you act towards outsiders. (Those who haven't yet received Jesus as
their savior.) They will be watching you to see if your behavior
matches your confession! If you say one thing and do another, they
will be turned off, thinking Christians are hypocrites. There is no
standard of integrity in the world system, so outsiders are looking
for something different, something real, from those who claim to
have a relationship with God.

If you wear a WWJD (what would Jesus do) shirt and then steal
something from your employer, you ruin your testimony. If you

witness to people about the love of God and then gossip or backbite, you are ruining God's good name and reputation in front of others.

Be careful to start obeying the things you read in God's Word and hear about in church. Many people can claim to know Christ, but refuse to obey what His Word teaches.

The Word of God declares in I John 2:4-5 "The man who says 'I know him,' but does not do what He commands is a liar and the truth is not in him. But if anyone obeys his Word, God's love is truly made complete in him. This is how we know we are in him: Whoever claims to live in him must walk as Jesus did." (NIV Translation)

It is not enough to display Christian symbols, or carry a Bible, or even to talk as if you are serving God. What God expects is obedience. There will be no power or victorious living for those who give lip service to the gospel.

For those who do their best to follow God's commands, and who depend on Him for daily forgiveness and cleansing, there is great joy, peace and power to overcome all sorts of difficulties. Those around you will notice you are living by higher standards, not giving in to the same sins that imprisoned you before you were saved. Your life will be a living Bible! Friends and family may or may not reject your new life, but if you live it before them with sincerity they will certainly see the power of the gospel at work.

Ask God for wisdom about how to speak and act around those who don't yet know Jesus Christ. The Holy Spirit will give you strategies about how to work with and witness to all different types of people!

When God offers you an opportunity to display His love to a non-believer, make the most of that moment. Don't be afraid to show them the 'new you.' They may judge you or criticize you, but in their hearts they are seeking God whether they realize it or not.

Allow the Lord to use you to be his lighthouse of love in your neighborhood, family or place of employment.

GET A BETTER GRIP by reading:
Romans 12:9-21   I John 3:9-10

What did God speak to me today through this chapter?

What action do I need to take in my life to apply what I have learned?

Chapter 43

What's in Your Mouth?
(Taming your tongue)
Colossians 4:6

"Be gracious in your speech. The goal is to bring out the best in others in a conversation, not put them down, and not cut them out."

Have you ever taken a good look at your tongue in the mirror? It's a really ugly and nasty looking organ. But if you didn't have your tongue, you could not talk or eat or swallow or drink. You could not form words or make clear sounds. Your tongue, as small and ugly as it is, plays a huge role in your life.

A different scripture in the book of James tells us that the tongue is like a little rudder on a big ship; though it's small it steers the whole ship! Your tongue can heal relationships or destroy them. It can curse or it can bless. Your tongue can drive a sharp business deal and sooth a wounded heart. Your tongue contains the power of life or death, and you can choose to control it so it brings life to people, or let it race out of control so it brings sorrow and pain to others. What comes out of your mouth is YOUR CHOICE.

What kinds of things do you talk about? Do you speak positively or negatively? Do you waste your words being critical? What kind of talk fills your day? Begin to examine yourself in this area.

You might find you will have to <u>retrain</u> yourself to speak a new language, the language of Love. Your old habits and ways of thinking and talking just won't cut it anymore.

Start by listening to yourself as you talk during an average day. Ask the Holy Spirit to show you things that are not pleasing, that are hurtful, and that will stop you from growing spiritually. You don't want anything, especially your own words, to stifle your growth in Christ. Then ask Him to help you discipline yourself to keep silent and HOLD your tongue! It is better to be quiet than to say hurtful, ungodly things. Then ask Jesus to give you <u>new</u> words to say about the situation and people you encounter.

These new words should be words of love, words that build people up and express compassion. Your new words need to be words of <u>faith</u>, which means you don't always immediately <u>see</u> the things you are speaking over a situation, but you believe that as you speak powerful words of love God uses those words to change the situation.

It is very important for you to begin focusing on positive thoughts and expressing positive words. Positive words will lift you out of gloomy attitudes and minister encouragement to those around you.

When you find yourself spitting out crude words, degrading and critical words, get a picture of a toilet in your mind. Take those words you've said, or are about to say, and flush them! That's where they belong.

The devil and your unrestrained flesh will attempt to forcefully introduce unwanted thoughts into your head, hoping you'll dwell on them long enough to finally shape them into words. You must refuse to entertain those thoughts, and refuse to speak them out. Just like junk food will bring sickness and disease to your body, unclean, negative and critical thoughts and words will bring disease to your entire life.

If you grab onto this truth it will change your life and the lives of the people around you. Don't allow your tongue to poison your life. Make it your goal to tame your tongue and make it serve up health, joy and peace to you and to your family. Even your enemies will notice a drastic difference in your conversations and wonder what got into you. Then you can say "It's Jesus! He got into me! And He's taming my tongue."

GET A BETTER GRIP by reading:
James 3:1-12   Proverbs 10:19-21   Proverbs 21:23

What did God speak to me today through this chapter?

What action do I need to take in my life to apply what I have learned?

Chapter 44

The Rewards of Loyalty
(Serving God by serving others well)
Colossians 4:7-8

> "My good friend Tychicus will tell you all about me. He's a
> trusted minister and companion in the service of the Master.
> I've sent him to you so that you would know how things are
> with us, and so he could encourage you in your faith."

Every pastor and spiritual leader would love a Tychicus. Here
was a man who had given his life to Christ, probably through
Paul's ministry, and then proceeded to become a true servant to
Paul.

The Apostle Paul's ministry was widespread. He wrote letters to
many different churches to encourage and instruct them to live for
Jesus. Tychicus hand delivered some of the letters Paul wrote, and
to do so required great sacrifice and effort. He had to cross at least 2
seas and 2 countries in order to carry Paul's letters to the churches.

Tychicus was a loyal helper and trusted assistant. When Paul
needed someone to represent him to other believers, he chose
Tychicus. I'm sure it was because Paul knew Tychicus could be
trusted to deliver the right messages in the right spirit. He was faithful
to represent Paul to others in the right way. In fact, he was so trustworthy that when pastors Titus and Timothy needed a temporary

replacement to preach for them, Paul recommended Tychicus.

The reward Tychicus received for his loyalty was promotion! In Paul's eyes, he was a valuable aid and a wonderful helper, a treasure of a man. Tychicus continued to receive rewards for his loyalty. People trusted him and knew that when he spoke he would be speaking things he had learned from the Apostle Paul. Believers received encouragement from him because they knew he wasn't speaking with selfish motives.

God wants us to use you in ministry, too. But first you must learn how to serve others and be a blessing to their ministries. If God calls you to help your pastor and your church by washing windows, then do it with a willing and joyful spirit. If God wants you to minister for your pastor by handing out bulletins on Sunday morning, then do it graciously! The people God promotes have passed the test of servanthood. They can be trusted with bigger things when they carry out small things diligently.

Don't be fooled into thinking that your gifts, abilities, or career successes automatically qualify you to be up front leading people spiritually. God doesn't allow puffed up, haughty or arrogant people to lead His church. He looks for the humble man, woman or child who is doing their duty and serving faithfully, without complaining or arguing. Then he exalts them to a place of leadership.

Determine to make yourself a blessing to your pastor and to your church. Ask God how you can serve them both. Do your duty faithfully and without grumbling. Find ways to encourage and bless the man or woman of God He has placed in spiritual authority over you.

God's church, (His body) does not operate the same way the business world operates, in a dog-eat-dog atmosphere, with those underneath coveting the job above them. God has designed His church to flow in the Holy Spirit, each Christian accomplishing the calling God has selected for them. When each one does his/her part, God's will is fulfilled.

God has given the church pastors to lead his people, and God's people are to support their pastor with prayers, their words, and their labor. The Kingdom of God will move forward unhindered when a pastor and the church are unified and operating in love and forgiveness towards one another. And the church body must recognize the God-given delegated authority of the pastor.

When God selected Moses to lead his people out of Egypt, God authorized and empowered Moses to be in charge. It was Moses' duty to seek God, hear His voice, and follow His directions. The people were then to follow wholeheartedly! Had the people of Israel done their part, they might have entered into the promised land. Instead, they wandered around a barren wilderness for 40 years, wishing they would have listened to God and His servant Moses.

God has called his people to be loyal to Him and to their pastor and church body. Loyalty means you are trustworthy, bonded together with church members, conscientious, supportive, earnest and obedient.

Being loyal requires you to speak honorably about your pastors, church leaders, and other members. When you disagree, you must pray about the issue, ask God if you are to approach leadership, and if so, you are to speak to them in love and with a self-controlled spirit.

When you are loyal to your church and your pastor, you are being loyal to God. If there is sin in the leadership or in the body, and you feel it is necessary to leave, do so without causing trouble. God is well able to deal with those He has selected for spiritual leadership.

The rewards of loyalty are tremendous. God will open doors of opportunity for you when He has tested you and found you trustworthy. You will gain the confidence of those you serve, and you will gain great joy and satisfaction yourself knowing you are pleasing God.

GET A BETTER GRIP by reading:
I Timothy 5:17-19   Hebrews 13:17   Numbers 16:1-35

What did God speak to me today through this chapter?

What action do I need to take in my life to apply what I have learned?

Chapter 45

From Bother to Brother
(The power of reconciliation)
Colossians 4:9

"And I've sent Onesimus with him. Onesimus is one of you, and has become such a trusted and dear brother! Together they'll bring you up to date on everything that has been going on here."

Onesimus was a thief and a runaway. He was a slave in the house of a man named Philemon, and one day he decided he was tired of being a slave, so he stole some material goods from Philemon and ran away to Rome.

In Rome, Onesimus happened to meet the Apostle Paul. Paul spoke to him about Jesus, and Onesimus believed. Instantly that put Onesimus in an interesting predicament. To serve Jesus, he knew he must go back to Philemon and repent, paying back all that he had stolen. But he also knew that he could be severely punished for running away, and so he must have been afraid. In those days, the penalty for being a runaway slave was often death.

Paul came to the rescue. He sat down and wrote Philemon a letter, appealing to him to take Onesimus back. He reported that Onesimus had become like a son to him, and that although he had formally been a <u>bother</u> and a useless servant, now he was a helpful <u>brother</u> in Christ. Paul even offered to pay for the things Onesimus had stolen, thereby softening Philemon's heart towards his former slave.

Since Philemon was a Christian man (he probably owned slaves before he was saved) Paul was confident that he would welcome Onesimus back as a new brother in the Lord, and would not mistreat or punish him (even though he deserved it).

When a person is saved, we who are already Christians have a duty and obligation to give each new Christian the benefit of the doubt and treat them as brothers and sisters. Even the people who have sinned against us or have caused us harm are worthy of new respect and a second chance. When Christ enters a person's heart, things begin to change. If we treat people as if there is no change, they will become discouraged and may fall away on account of us. When we have an opportunity to restore a former <u>bother</u> and treat him/her like a <u>brother,</u> we should do our duty and treat them with love and encouragement. Jesus will help us do what is hard to do in our own strength.

If a person is not sincere about their walk with Christ that will become clear soon enough, and then you may take scriptural action to deal with their deceitfulness.

Remember Jesus' example to us with Peter. Even though Peter denied Jesus 3 times, Jesus accepted him back and restored him. When we respond like Christ we will be rewarded for living as Jesus did.

GET A BETTER GRIP by reading:
Philemon 8-19   John 21:15-19

What did God speak to me today through this chapter?

What action do I need to take to apply what I have learned?

Chapter 46

Making New Friends
Colossians 4:10

"Aristarchus, who is in jail here with me, sends greetings"

There are people who enjoy being your friend when you have plenty of money. There are folks who will hang around as long as you will party with them. There are those who call themselves 'friends' who would 'stick it to you' if it was in their best interest.

And then there is that rare person who becomes a true friend, one who is reliable and who loves you just because you are <u>you</u>. That is the type of friend Paul found in Aristarchus.

It seems Aristarchus was with Paul whenever Paul was in difficult situations. When there was a riot in the city of Ephesus because of Paul's teachings, Aristarchus was right there with the Apostle. He was even seized by the furious mob, risking his life because of Paul.

Now that Paul was in prison, this faithful friend Aristarchus willingly allowed himself to be imprisoned also in order to meet Paul's needs. Wow. Now that's incredible.

When you become a Christian, you must re-learn what true friendship is all about. Maybe you have had bad experiences with friends in your past, or maybe you have been a poor friend to others. In either case, God wants you to understand what it means to be a 'friend.'

Being a friend means loving someone with a selfless love. You want the best for that person, and you want to see them prosper and succeed. Instead of being jealous of their achievements you will want to rejoice that they are doing well!

Godly friendships are built on healthy activities (activities that are good for your body, mind and spirit). Perhaps in the past your friendships revolved around drugs, sexual sin and other unhealthy involvements. Now it's time to move beyond those so-called friendships! God wants to surround you with friends who will encourage you spiritually and help build you into a dynamic force for God.

A godly friend will guard your reputation, thinking and speaking the best about you in front of other people.

A true friend sticks close by when things are going badly for you. He/she is willing to unselfishly go out of his/her way to see that you are encouraged and comforted.

The friends God wants for you will not lead you into temptation, but will help deliver you when you face evil. A true blue buddy will pray with you and fight spiritual battles on your behalf!

If you are a woman, God wants you to pursue godly female companions. If you are a male, you need to seek after men of God who can mentor you in the faith. If you are married, it is dangerous to pursue close friendships with a person of the opposite sex. The devil wants to set you up for disaster, and God wants you to be free from temptation. Go after friendships and mentoring relationships with godly people of your same gender.

Aristarchus is an awesome example of a true friend. You too, can experience the joy of true friendship as you focus on <u>being</u> a good friend as well as pursuing godly friendships.

GET A BETTER GRIP by reading:
Proverbs 17:17   John 15:13

What did God speak to me today through this chapter?

What action do I need to take in my life to apply what I have learned?

Chapter 47

Choosing a Church
Colossians 4:12-13

"Epaphras, who is one of you, says hello. What a trooper he has been! He's been tireless in his prayers for you, praying that you'll stand firm, mature and confident in everything God wants you to do. I've watched him closely, and can report on how hard he has worked for you and for those in Laodicea and Hierapolis."

Have you been flipping through the yellow pages looking for just the right church? Have you visited several churches, and you still don't know where to go? It can be confusing trying to discern in which 'family of God' you belong! But it's not as hard as it seems.

First of all, understand that becoming involved in a church is not an option, it's a command in the Bible and absolutely essential for your spiritual growth and development.

Watching church on T.V. alone is not God's plan for your life. T.V. church is supplemental, helping to minister to those who have never been to church or who cannot attend for health reasons.

Staying home and reading the Bible won't cut it. That's a cop out! God has a powerful plan for your life that includes input from other believers. Stay-at-home Christians are robbing themselves of

God's best for their life, and robbing God of ministry involvement.

Becoming part of a local church puts you in the company of fellow believers. Christians need other Christians to grow strong!

So, what are the characteristics you need to look for when you are searching for a church home?

1. Choose a church that believes the Bible is the inspired Word of God, that it is <u>completely true</u> and cannot be changed at man's whim. Make certain the Bible they use is one with 39 books in the Old Testament, 27 in the New Testament, and one that does not distort the original language in order to become culturally or politically correct.

2. Choose a church that believes Jesus Christ is the only son of God and the only means by which we can be saved. They must freely confess that Jesus was born of a virgin, lived a sinless life, died on the cross as a substitute for our sins, was resurrected 3 days later and now sits at the right hand of God in heaven.

3. Choose a church that believes in One True God made up of three persons: The Father, The Son and the Holy Spirit. (Sort of like the egg-thing: the shell, the yolk, and the white are all one egg in 3 distinct parts.)

4. Choose a church that reaches out to the lost and to hurting people to bring them to Jesus. A healthy church will have a great missions program to reach people in their community, their country, and the world.

5. Choose a church whose pastor preaches messages from God's Word which causes you to grow spiritually.

6. Choose a church that teaches and practices holy living. God is a holy God, and desires that His people pursue righteous and holy living. The pastor, church leaders, elders, and the people as a whole will display a modest and clean spirit.

7. Choose a church that believes people are born into sin and must receive Jesus Christ as savior in order to be forgiven and enter heaven when they die.

8. Choose a church that teaches and preaches the truth of a final judgment day when those in Christ will be rewarded for their faith and works, and those who've rejected Him will have selected to spend their eternity apart from God in hell.

9. Choose a church where the love of God is manifested in the behavior, teachings, and attitudes of the members.

10. Choose a church that stays focused on God's Word as the ABSOLUTE TRUTH no matter what sins are flaunted, displayed and accepted in the culture at large.

When you are searching for a church, it is important to make sure that the pastor has many of the same characteristics that Epaphras had. Epaphras was the pastor of the church of the Colossians. He was an obvious servant of Jesus, a man of prayer who encouraged and taught his people to pray and trust God. People who sat under his ministry became confident in their walk with God.

Epaphras taught the Word and the church developed maturity and understood God's will. He taught them how to stand firm in the Christian life and resist doing things the world's way. He was also a hard worker in ministry, leading by example.

Epaphras had earned Paul's respect, so we know that Epaphras respected and honored the spiritual authority God had placed over him. That typically means a man is humble and teachable, willing to be subject and accountable to others.

When you are searching for a church, make certain that all of these characteristics are present before you become involved. It is a safety precaution for you and prevents you from becoming involved with deceivers, money-hungry liars and cults of all kinds.

When you begin attending a church, pay your tithes (10% of your income), which is commanded in God's Word. (Malachi 3:6-

11, Matthew 23:23) The tithes were ordered by God to provide for the support of the ministry and those who minister. They are not an option, either! God has promised to bless you incredibly if you give him the first part 10% of your paycheck. God declares that He will prove Himself faithful to you if you trust Him and pay your tithes. Remember, God is SO generous; He gives you 90% to keep!

It is also essential for you to become involved in a ministry, and be faithful in attendance and support. Speak well of your good pastor, for if he is a man like Epaphras, he is worthy of your honor and blessing.

Now you're ready! Ask God to lead you to the wonderful church you are to support with your encouragement, your work and your finances.

GET A BETTER GRIP by reading:
Psalm 35:18   Hebrews 10:25

What did God speak to me today through this chapter?

What action do I need to take in my life to apply what I have learned?

Chapter 48

You Don't Have To Be a Star to Be in His Show
(God uses available and faithful people)
Colossians 4:14

"Luke, good friend and physician, and Demas both send greetings."

Hollywood has got to be a rough place to try to find work! Unless you are a big name, it's next to impossible to be considered for a starring role in a high dollar film. Many talented actors and actresses have been cast aside because they aren't considered 'stars.'

Man, aren't you glad God doesn't work that way! You don't have to be famous, or good-looking, or particularly talented to be used to glorify and build God's kingdom on earth. All you have to be is <u>available</u>! Your educational background, your family name, and the amount of money you make aren't qualifications to be used powerfully in God's spiritual kingdom. God uses those who are humble, and the Bible says that those people will someday shine like the stars forever and ever! (Daniel 12:3)

The 'Luke' mentioned in the above scripture was a humble, spiritually sensitive doctor. He also happened to be an educated, intellectual man with superb writing skills. When he gave his heart to Jesus Christ, his entire life changed. He was still a doctor, but God gave his life's work eternal purpose and meaning. He simply wanted to be used by God to share the good news of Jesus Christ. You can be used greatly in God's kingdom, just like Luke was!

Thousands of people each year give their lives to Jesus. And He has a special life-plan for each person. In fact, the Bible says that <u>all</u> the days ordained for you were written in His book even before one of them came to be. It also says that God knows the plans He has for you, plans to make you a success and not harm you!

If you have been trained to be a teacher or a lawyer or a businessman, God can use your skills to impact people with the good news of God's love for them. If you are a brick layer or a stay-at-home mom or a truck driver, God wants to use you in a mighty way to reach out to people that you have contact with every day.

The most exciting part about being a Christian is that God uses us, with all our faults and weaknesses, to tell others about the mercy and compassion of Jesus. He doesn't say we have to all be preachers to share God's message. He wants to use us and the talents we have (and those we don't!) to reach all types of people.

Luke was a doctor who lived in the time of Christ. I'm certain that he could have used his knowledge and position to gain money and prestige for himself. But when he came to know Jesus as his personal savior, God gave him another emphasis. Even though he continued doctoring, Luke obeyed God by writing the historical accounts of Jesus' life and the lives and actions of the apostles. Those accounts are in the Bible, (the book of Luke and the book of Acts.) Those books have impacted people all over the world!

You don't have to give up your life's work to be used by God. (Unless of course you were a drug dealer or a criminal!) Just make yourself available to Him and He will instruct you how to let your light shine for Him. Even if the people or the rules in your workplace seem to restrict sharing the gospel, God will give you a way to demonstrate His love.

Allow God access to your professional life! Let Him direct your steps and give you supernatural wisdom. You'll be amazed how He uses your life for His glory. And don't allow yourself to say "God, choose someone else who is more talented in this area than I am," because God chooses whom He wishes!

If he calls you to do a task for Him, He will enable you to carry it out with success. Many times God uses the person who doesn't understand how to go about carrying out a mission, because they are humble and teachable. God is able to lead that kind of person.

You don't have to be a star to be in His show. Just show up! And be faithful.

GET A BETTER GRIP by reading:
Jeremiah 29:11   Psalm 139:13-16

What did God speak to me today through this chapter?

What action do I need to take in my life to apply what I have learned?

Chapter 49

Falling Out of Love with Jesus
(Dealing with temptation)
Colossians 4:14, 2 Timothy 4:10, Philemon 24

"Luke, good friend and physician, and Demas both send greetings."

"Demas, chasing fads, went off to Thessalonica and left me here."

When God saved you, He did a powerful work! He cleansed you from your sin through the awful suffering of His son Jesus. Not only does God have the power to <u>save </u>you, but He also has the power to <u>keep</u> you close to Him, too.

The only way for you to escape God's great love and protection would be for you to <u>willingly</u> decide to turn back to a life of sin.

Demas was a faithful friend to the Apostle Paul for a long time. He was with Paul both times Paul was thrown in prison. But something changed in Demas' life. Somewhere along the line Demas allowed his thoughts to linger on things in the world that looked appetizing. He may have let his mind wander to an old girlfriend or an old way of life or a new religious fad. Soon, Demas found himself thinking that those things looked pretty exciting and tempting! And before he even realized what was happening to him, Demas began to turn away from his new life in Christ.

He deserted the Apostle Paul and he deserted the ministry God had given him. Demas gave up everything that was important to him because he began to love the things of the world again.

What are the 'things of the world?' Anything that fulfills the lusting of our human desires and does not bring about God's will in our lives. These are the things that try to woo us away from our personal friendship with Jesus. They appear tantalizing and pleasurable, but in the end those things will destroy us.

We have the right to choose. God didn't create us to be machines who obey Him at the flip of a switch. We can choose to serve Him and stay close to Him or we can choose to turn back to a life of sin and rebellion. The end result of a rebellious life is eternity in hell, because the Bible says:

"If we deliberately keep on sinning after we have received the knowledge of the truth, no sacrifice for sins is left, but only a fearful expectation of judgment and of raging fire." (Hebrews 10:26 NIV)

However, if we remain in Him, <u>choosing</u> to live our lives in obedience to His commands, God <u>promises</u> that He is able to keep us from falling! He only requires that we be willing and obedient, and He will do the rest to help us and rescue us from temptation and sin.

Don't be a Demas! Never turn away from God and His plans for you. You will never find true happiness, joy and peace apart from God's love. Close your eyes and your ears to satan's seductive enticements. Everything you have been searching for you will find in Christ!

What do we know about temptation that will help us battle against it?

1) Jesus told us "Get up and pray so that you will not fall into temptation." Luke 22:46 In the morning, before you face anything or anyone, pray for deliverance from temptation. Ask the Lord Jesus to help you avoid tempting situations.

2) God promises to be faithful to us, not allowing tempting situations to overpower us. His Word says:

"No temptation has seized you except what is common to man. And God is faithful, he will not let you be tempted beyond what you can bear. But when you are tempted, he will also provide a way out so that you can stand up under it." I Corinthians 10:13

3) Temptation causes suffering, bringing condemnation and guilt. When we are tempted, we often feel like we have failed the Lord. But being tempted and giving in to temptation are very different things. Every Christian will be tempted throughout the course of their lifetime. However, Jesus promised to help us in these moments of temptation to say <u>NO!</u> to sin and walk away. When we are successful in resisting temptation, assurance and peace will flood our souls. And when we fail and fall into temptation, it is important to immediately repent and get back on track, not allowing satan to have one more inch of territory.

God's Word carries this promise for all of us: "Because He Himself suffered when he was temped, he is able to help those who are being tempted." Hebrews 2:18

GET A BETTER GRIP by reading:
Jude 24   Hebrews 10:19-31   John 15:1-12

What did God speak to me today through this chapter?

What action do I need to take in my life to apply what I have learned?

Chapter 50

Finishing Strong

Colossians 4:17-18

"... tell Archippus, "Do your best in the job you received from the Master. Do your very best."

Maybe you've seen the popular billboard with a picture of a U.S. Marine and the caption "Pain is weakness leaving your body." The photo captures the image of a man who knows what hard work and sacrifice are all about.

God has assigned you an important task in His kingdom. Perhaps you have already discovered that task and are making great strides forward. If you have not found the place of ministry God has ordained for you, keep asking Him to reveal it to you. He will certainly show you!

Once you start ministering with God, you'll discover you need perseverance and patience, because doing kingdom work isn't for wimps!

Every believer would love to see powerful and dynamic supernatural events occur in the ministry God has selected for them. However, more often you simply have to work very hard, keep your hopes very high, and draw your daily strength from Jesus Christ!

You are not 'working for God.' I like the way Henry Blackably describes ministry in his book "Experiencing God:" we join God in HIS work!

At times you will feel like you are burning out. At moments you will be disappointed with the way a ministry event or ministry relationship turned out. You might even wrestle with feelings of inadequacy if you make the mistake of comparing yourself with another person ministering in the same field.

At that point it is wise to remember that God wants us to finish strong. Sure, there will be hard places in our walk with God and in the ministry task He's selected for us, but He has ordained those times so the weak places in our lives can be made strong.

The earthly ministry we share with God is passing away. Sooner or later all your best laid plans and goals will melt into eternity. You must concentrate on fixing your heart on your personal relationship with Jesus, and not falling in love with the ministry. Jesus always wants to be your first love!

When you remain closely connected with Jesus, you will finish your life and ministry on earth in strength and victory. And the hard times, like Paul's months as a prisoner in chains, will disappear like the morning mist.

Make it your highest goal to serve God faithfully to the end of your life. Whether He asks you to be in the spotlight or in the shadows, shoot for a disciplined daily walk with your Master.

Allow no sin, no temptation and no human being to stand in the way of your total commitment to Jesus Christ. Don't let yourself be a satanic statistic! Too many believers start their faith-life with a bang and end with a whimper. Usually they have been sidelined because they have not determined ahead of time they are going to make right, godly choices when confronted with evil.

Keep your life on earth in perspective. Soon, you will see Christ face-to-face. All your troubles will seem light and distant compared to the fantastic joy of living in His presence for eternity.

Work with all the energy the Holy Spirit gives you, laboring in the area of ministry to which God has anointed you. And keep your eyes peeled on the eastern sky, for Jesus will appear with the angels to snatch you away from this world to be with Him forever.

GET A BETTER GRIP by reading:
I Peter 4:1-11   2 Corinthians 4:1-2   2 Corinthians 6:3-10

What did God speak to me today through this chapter?

What action do I need to take in my life to apply what I have learned?